Child's identification card bearing the Nazi coat of arms,
issued to Marion Blumenthal, age three and a half,
in Hoya, Germany, on June 10, 1938

LILA PERL AND
MARION BLUMENTHAL LAZAN

Four Perfect Pebbles

A TRUE STORY OF THE HOLOCAUST

 Greenwillow Books

An Imprint of HarperCollins*Publishers*

United States Holocaust Memorial Museum: 37 top, 37 bottom (William O. McWorkman), 38 top and center; National Archives: 38 bottom, 83 top and bottom; Yad Vashem: 40 bottom, 44 bottom; YIVO: 42 bottom. All other photographs are supplied by Marion Blumenthal Lazan.

Four Perfect Pebbles: A True Story of the Holocaust

The text of this book is set in Bembo Infant MT Std.

Library of Congress Control Number: 2016946899
ISBN 978-0-06-248996-8 (twentieth anniversary paperback)
22 23 24 25 26 LBC 18 17 16 15 14

 Greenwillow Books

Revised paperback edition, 2016

To Joan Newman, to whom I am deeply grateful for the privilege of having met Marion Blumenthal Lazan.

—L. P.

To my mother, Ruth Blumenthal Meyberg, who carried the full burden and whose love and perseverance saw us through, and to my husband, Nathaniel, whose deep devotion has made the perpetuation of our heritage possible. And in memory of my father, Walter Blumenthal, who would have derived great joy and fulfillment from his three grandchildren—David, Susan, and Michael— and nine great-grandchildren—Arielle, Joshua, Gavriel, Dahlia, Yoav, Jordan Erica, Hunter, Ian, and Kasey Rose.

To all those who have known adversity and despair, I offer my belief that out of darkness can come light.

—M. B. L.

CONTENTS

PROLOGUE

This is the story of a family—a mother and father and their two young children—who became trapped in Hitler's Germany. They managed eventually to leave that country for Holland, where they were soon again caught in the Nazis' web, and their situation grew even more serious. For in the final years of World War II, when the Holocaust reached its most feverish pitch, the four members of the Blumenthal family were returned to Germany.

During their ordeal, lasting six and a half years, the Blumenthals lived in refugee, transit, and prison camps that included Westerbork in Holland and the notorious concentration camp at Bergen-Belsen in Germany.

Bergen-Belsen was the camp to which Anne Frank and her sister, Margot, were transported in October 1944. The two girls, aged fifteen and nineteen, died there of typhus in March 1945. It was in the very same section of Bergen-Belsen that the Blumenthal family remained imprisoned from February 1944 to April 1945.

Marion Blumenthal, the younger of the two children, was nine years old when she arrived there. Her brother, Albert, was eleven.

The British troops who liberated Bergen-Belsen on April 15, 1945, wrote of its "indescribable" horrors. "Piles of corpses" lay unburied everywhere, while those who still breathed were "little more than living skeletons." The entire camp population was infested with lice. Those prisoners who had not already succumbed were the dying victims of typhus and other epidemic diseases, starvation, exposure, and neglect.

The Blumenthals, however, were not among the deeply suffering prisoners who might have benefited from the British capture of Bergen-Belsen on April 15. Six days earlier they had been marched to the camp's loading platform and placed aboard a train of cattle cars headed east in the direction of the dreaded Auschwitz extermination camp. For two weeks the "death train," so named for the many passengers who died of typhus, made its tortuous way across Nazi Germany. When liberation came at last, it was at the hands of Russian troops who had little to offer those who staggered weakly from the train.

As a grown woman Marion Blumenthal Lazan recalls the events that shaped her youth. She tells of the four years she spent with her family in Holland's Westerbork, of her terrified arrival in Bergen-Belsen and what it was like to live through the long chain of days behind its barbed-wire fences, and of the struggles of her teenage years of postwar Europe and America.

Invaluable details and documentation have also been supplied by her mother, Ruth Blumenthal Meyberg, and her brother, Albert Blumenthal. The inner strength and enduring spirit of the members of this family make it possible for all of us to become witnesses to an evil that, sadly, must remain forever in human memory.

CHAPTER 1

"Four Perfect Pebbles"

Long before dawn crept through the windows of the wooden barrack, Marion stirred in Mama's arms. She had slept this way, wrapped in her mother's warmth, for many weeks now, ever since her family had arrived at the concentration camp at Bergen-Belsen in northwestern Germany.

All around her were the sounds of the other women and children, lying in the three-decker bunks that ran the length of the barrack. As Marion came awake, the muffled noises sharpened. There were gasps and moans, rattling coughs, and short, piercing cries. And there was the ever-present stench of unwashed bodies, disease, and death.

Hardly a morning passed without some of the prisoners no longer able to rise from their thin straw mattresses. When the guards came to round up the women and children for roll call, they stopped briefly to examine the unmoving forms. Later those who had died in the night would be tumbled from their bunks onto crude stretchers, and their bodies taken away to be burned or buried in mass graves. Soon new prisoners would arrive to take their places. As many as six hundred would be crowded into barracks meant to hold a hundred.

Mama nudged Marion. "Get up, *Liebling*. It's time."

As soon as Mama withdrew her arms, thin as they had become, the warmth vanished, and the chill of the unheated room gripped Marion's nine-year-old body. Cold and hunger. In her first weeks at Bergen-Belsen, Marion had been unable to decide which was worse. Soon, however, the constant gnawing sensation in her belly began to vanish. Her stomach accustomed itself to the daily ration of a chunk of black bread and a cup of watery turnip soup, and its capacity shrank. But the bitter chill of the long German winter went on and on.

On one of her earliest days in the camp Marion had actually believed that she saw a wagonload of firewood approaching. Perhaps it would stop in front of the barrack and some logs would be fed into the empty stove that was supposed to heat the entire room, for a few hours of glorious warmth. But she had been horribly mistaken. The wagon trundled past, and a closer look told her that it was filled not with firewood but with the naked, sticklike bodies of dead prisoners.

As on all winter mornings, getting dressed in the predawn grayness took no time at all. Marion had slept in just about everything she owned. All she had to do was to put her arms through the sleeves of the tattered coat that she had used as an extra covering under the coarse, thin blanket the camp provided.

Soon the cries of the Kapos (*Kameradshaftspolizei*, or police aides)—privileged prisoners who served as guards—were heard as they moved from barrack to barrack.

"Zum Appell! Appell! Raus, Juden!"

Marion and Mama must now find a way to relieve themselves before hurrying to the large square, with its watchtower and armed guards, where the daily *Appell*, or roll call, took place. There was not always time to visit the communal outhouse, about a block away from the barrack. The toilets in the outhouse were simply a long wooden bench with holes in it, suspended over a trench. There was no water to flush away the waste, no toilet paper, and, of course, no privacy.

Some mornings, Marion and Mama and the other prisoners had to use whatever receptacles they owned as night buckets— even the very mugs or bowls in which they received their daily rations. Before leaving the barrack for *Appell*, the prisoners had to make sure the room was clean, the floor swept, and their beds made. Each inmate stood in front of her bunk for inspection. If the blankets were not tucked neatly enough around the sagging straw mattresses, punishments were meted out. The slightest infraction could mean losing one's bread ration for the day.

Roll call was held twice a day, at six in the morning and again after the prisoners had returned from their work assignments. It was held in winter and summer, in ice and snow, in rain and mud. If a single person was missing because of sickness, death, or an attempted escape, all the prisoners were made to stand at attention, in rows of five, for hours—even for a whole day— without food or water or any way to relieve themselves.

Some prisoners did try to escape, but very few succeeded. Each section of the camp was surrounded by a high fence of barbed wire. The fence was charged with electricity and had pictures of death's-heads posted on it as a warning. Prisoners who attempted to scale the fence were electrocuted. Others who tried to escape while on a work detail, outside the fenced areas, were almost always caught by the watchful eyes of the armed guards, by keen-nosed police dogs, or at night by sweeping searchlights.

Marion hoped, as she did every morning, that the roll call in the square would be over as quickly as possible. Then, after dismissal, there might be a few moments to see Papa and her eleven-year-old brother, Albert, who were imprisoned in separate barracks in the men's section.

In Westerbork, the Dutch camp where the family had lived before, all four of them had been housed in a crude but private quarters. However, no such arrangement existed for any of the prisoners in Bergen-Belsen. Actually they were told they should consider themselves "lucky" to be in the section of the camp known as the *Sternlager*, or Star Camp. Here male and female prisoners were allowed to meet briefly during the day. Also, they could dress in their own clothes instead of striped prison uniforms. But of course, they must wear the yellow Star of David high up on the left side of the chest, as they had been forced to do for many years now. In the center of the six-pointed star the word *Jude* (German for "Jew") was inscribed in black.

Today, possibly because of the icy temperature, the barracks guards had begun reporting their head counts quickly. There were two prisoners missing. But they had already been found. They had "run into the wires" sometime during the night. This was the term the Kapos used to describe the act of committing suicide when prisoners died by hurling themselves against the electrified barbed-wire fences.

In just under one hour the roll call had been completed. Already Marion and Mama had spotted Albert and Papa across the frozen ground of the square. Now the entire family came together in a hasty, wordless embrace, for there was never much time.

At once Papa began to push into Mama's hands the extra rations he had managed to trade for cigarettes. In the weeks since the family had come to Bergen-Belsen, the male prisoners in the *Sternlager* had been receiving a small number of cigarettes once every few days. Papa, who did not smoke, immediately went about exchanging his cigarettes with other prisoners for bits of food, such as a small chunk of bread, a turnip, or even a potato. Mama, after making sure that Papa had kept enough for himself and Albert, squirreled these items away for herself and Marion.

Albert, too, usually had a small horde of secret treasure. He carefully collected the tobacco from partially smoked cigarette butts and made his own trades to get extra rations.

Marion had brought along her own secret treasure this morning, but hers was not anything to eat. She felt in her coat pocket to make sure the three pebbles were still there. There she carefully drew them out and opened her palm for Albert to see.

Albert, who seemed to be growing taller and more skeletal every day, looked down at Marion's hand. "Yes, I see," he said with a wan smile. "That again."

"*That* again." Marion mimicked him. Her deep-set eyes grew fiery. "Look closely. I have these three pebbles, exactly matching. Today I will find the fourth. I suppose you think I'm silly."

"No, no." Albert calmed her. He had always been the soothing, protective child. Marion was the excitable one.

"Four perfect pebbles," Marion said proudly, watching her own breath form a mist in the frosty air. "One for each one of us. You'll see. I'll show you the fourth one tomorrow."

Albert placed a hand on her shoulder. "Yes, of course."

Marion flashed him a look, part love, part impatience. Big brothers were all the same. Time and again Albert told her that there could be no such thing as even *two* perfectly matching pebbles. Pebbles were like snowflakes. Every single one was different from every other one.

But Marion ignored such scientific reasoning. She had

a fixed idea, one that was important for her to hold on to. If she could find four pebbles of almost exactly the same size and shape, it meant that her family could remain whole. Mama and Papa and she and Albert would survive Bergen-Belsen. The four of them might even survive the Nazis' attempt to destroy every last Jew in Europe.

Over and over Marion had collected such pebbles in groups of four, terrifying herself when she could find only two or three and not a fourth that matched. A foolish pastime? A superstition? Perhaps. But the sets of pebbles were her lucky charms, and they gave her a purpose.

Searching for a complete set was a way to fill the succession of empty days. Every day of Bergen-Belsen was the same, with nothing to do but stand at roll call and worry about when Mama would reappear from her work detail. In Westerbork, where they had lived for the past four years, some of the camp inmates taught informal classes. But here there was no schooling or even any work for a child of nine.

There was only Marion's self-invented game. It was her way of keeping her family together. It was also a way of linking a past she could vaguely remember with a future that she could hardly imagine.

How *had* Marion's family become caught in the Nazis' trap? Why had Papa's carefully thought-out plans to escape from Germany failed? When, in fact, had all their troubles started?

Marion was too young to remember having lived the beginning of the story. But Mama remembered. She knew it all, and she would tell it to Marion as they lay whispering in their bunk at night.

As Mama told it, their family story sounded like a fairy tale that grew more and more frightening as it went on. Its ending had not been written yet. But it did have a fairly happy beginning. "Of course, you don't remember"—Mama would sigh as she drew the covers more tightly around them—"when you were just a baby in that small town in Germany. . . ."

CHAPTER 2

"A Small Town in Germany"

Hoya. That was the name of the town where Marion had lived for the first four years of her life. It lies on the Weser River in northwestern Germany, about halfway between the cities of Hanover and Bremen. Like many of the old towns along the river, its streets were lined with pointy-roofed merchants' houses, for the Weser was an outlet to the North Sea.

Mama often recalled how as a young woman of twenty she'd taken a very long train ride across northern Germany to "seek her future" and ended up in, of all places, Hoya.

Mama, who was born Ruth Moses, was the eldest of five

daughters of a German-Jewish family living near the city of Tilsit, in far-off East Prussia. Today Tilsit, renamed Sovetsk, is part of Russia. "I wanted to get out of that small place," she told her children. "So I answered an ad in the newspaper for a job as a bookkeeper. The first work I got was in Brakel, a place in Westphalia, to the south of here. But after a time I saw an ad for a better job, in a shoe store in Hoya. Hoya was even smaller than Brakel. And much, much smaller than Tilsit. It had only three thousand people and exactly forty-four Jews. But I liked it, so I stayed."

There was more to Mama's story than that. After working just two weeks in the Blumenthals' family business in Hoya, she received a proposal of marriage from their son, Walter. And in December 1931, when Ruth was twenty-three and Walter was thirty-five, the couple married. Their first child, Albert, was born on October 11, 1932. Marion was born two years later, on December 20, 1934.

Lini and Max Blumenthal, Marion's grandparents whom she knew as Oma and Opa, were as much a part of her early memories as were her parents and her brother. The older Blumenthals lived on the second floor of a tall, sturdily built house in the town center. Marion's family lived on the third floor. On the first, or ground, floor was the store itself, where Papa and Opa sold shoes and men's and boys' clothing and where Mama continued her bookkeeping and secretarial duties.

Oma cared for Albert and Marion and cooked the evening meal, for which the entire family gathered. While Marion, the baby of the family, was being rocked to sleep, the grown-ups sat around the table and talked. "We talked," Mama remembered, "about the store, about the events of the day, and mostly about that man Hitler."

"That man Hitler." He had been around for ten years or more by the early 1930s, when Albert and Marion were born. As the leader of the National Socialist German Workers' party— the Nazi party, for short (from *Nazional*, the German word for National)—he ranted against Communists, Jews, and gypsies, and against Slavic peoples, such as Poles and Russians, all of whom he considered inferior. He also denounced any Germans who were crippled, deformed, or mentally ill as being unworthy of existence.

Such nonsense, most people thought at first. The man was nothing more than a political crackpot with a small band of followers. In 1923 he had served nine months in jail after a crazed attempt to overthrow the government. His Nazi party was only one of many political parties that were represented by popular vote in the Reichstag, the lower house of the German parliament.

Yet by 1930 the Nazi party had gained an alarming number of deputies in the Reichstag. In a little more than a year its representatives had increased from 12 to 107. And two years later, in 1932, the Nazi party, with 37 percent of the vote, was the largest in Germany. Too splintered politically to form a united front against the Nazis, the other parties had become small and helpless.

Why, the Blumenthals debated around their family dinner table, had this frightening development taken place? One didn't have to look far for the answer. Economic conditions in Germany had been very bad ever since the defeat of the fatherland in the Great War of 1914–1918. And the worldwide depression that hit in 1929 had only made things worse.

Hitler insisted that he had the remedy for all of Germany's woes. Through his frequent public speeches at massive Nazi-sponsored rallies, he made his message clear. He would restore Germany's honor, increase its territory, and bring back its lost prosperity. His attacks on its "enemies within," especially the Jews, grew more and more frenzied. Once again the long-smoldering hatred of the Jews, known as anti-Semitism—one of the oldest prejudices in the world—was fanned into flames.

In one way it seemed strange that Hitler should pick on Germany's Jews, because there were so few of them. They numbered only about 500,000 in a population of 67 million, less than 1 percent of the German citizenry. But in spite of being a minority, they were remarkably visible on the German scene.

True, Jews didn't run the giant industries of Germany, such as Krupp, Farben, or Siemens. Nor did many Jews hold high political offices. But they were involved in businesses and professions, such as banking, merchandising, publishing, medicine, science, and the arts. In the capital city of Berlin, where about one-third of Germany's Jews lived, the major department stores were Jewish-owned: Wertheim, Hermann Teitz, N. Israel, and the famed KaDeWe, or Kaufhaus des Westens. Whatever abilities, talents, influence, or wealth the Jews of Germany possessed were seen as a threat by the Nazis.

Today the year that is remembered as the beginning of official racist activity in Germany is 1933. On January 30 Adolf Hitler, as the leader of the majority party, was appointed chancellor, or prime minister, by Germany's president, the aged Paul von

Hindenburg. The chancellor lost no time in putting his new powers to work. On April 1 he ordered a nationwide boycott of all Jewish-owned businesses. Signs reading DON'T BUY FROM JEWS were posted on shopwindows in major cities and in towns large and small. Hitler's order was enforced by the presence of brown-uniformed Nazi storm troopers who blocked the entrances to Jewish-owned stores, medical offices, and law firms.

"Did we find this surprising?" Mama remarked as she recalled the 1933 boycott. "Yes, in a way. How could it be that people in that small town of Hoya would turn away from us so quickly? Walter's parents had been in business there since 1894. They always gave good service and value and were highly respected by their customers from both the town and the surrounding countryside.

"Walter grew up in that town. In 1914, at the age of seventeen, he volunteered for the German Army. He served his country in the Great War for four years and was awarded the medal of honor known as the Iron Cross. But all this was immediately forgotten when Hitler took power. As early as April 1933, a few days after the Jewish boycott began, children ran through the street throwing stones at Albert's baby carriage."

As the boycott continued, business dropped off at the store.

So Walter bought a small car and began to make deliveries to people in the town and on the farms. "Our old customers still wanted the merchandise we sold," Mama explained, "but they were afraid to be seen entering the store."

The discussions around the Blumenthals' dinner table grew more intense. Walter thought that the family should make plans to leave Germany at once. But Oma and Opa, already elderly, could not imagine leaving the business and moving away. "You will see," the older Blumenthals counseled. "This Hitler won't last. Before long things will come back to normal."

"Back to normal," Mama repeated bitterly. "How could that happen? The very next year, in 1934, the elderly President von Hindenburg died and Hitler became both chancellor *and* president of Germany, its supreme leader, *der Führer*."

Ruth Blumenthal had been right. The future held no real hope for improvement. Already, children, like those who had stoned Albert's baby carriage, were being groomed for the Hitler Youth. Even three-year-olds were given Nazi banners to wave. The flag featured a bold black swastika inside a white circle, surrounded by a bright red field. The Nazi swastika, based on a symbol used by many different ancient peoples, was a cross with its arms extended at right angles in a clockwise direction.

German schoolchildren wearing uniforms with swastika armbands were soon organized into formal groups and trained in the Nazi creed. A favorite marching song of the Hitler Youth of 1934 contained the words:

Und wenn das Judenblut vom Messer spritzt,
Dann geht's nochmal so gut!
[And when Jewish blood spurts from the knife,
Then things will go well again!]

The following year Hitler made anti-Semitism part of German law. The so-called Nuremberg Laws of September 15, 1935, were passed by the Reichstag at its meeting in the southern German city of Nuremberg. These rulings stripped Jews of their German citizenship and prohibited marriage between Jews and non-Jewish or other "pure" Germans, known as Aryans. Germany's Jews were now completely cut off from any hope of receiving just treatment under the law.

The boycott, which aimed at destroying all Jewish businesses in Germany, had, of course, continued. At the same time non-Jewish firms were pressured to dismiss their Jewish employees. Signs in shopwindows, advertising for help, clearly read JEWS NOT WANTED.

With the takeover of Jewish businesses and jobs, properties and bank accounts, Germany's economy was already beginning to improve. But Hitler planned to go much further. Germany, he declared, was to become *Judenrein*, or totally free of Jews. Meantime, disobedience or even the suspicion that a Jew was not complying with the laws could lead to beatings, arrests, imprisonment, and even death. Not all Germans agreed with the racial policies of the Nazis. But few had the courage to defy the iron rule of Hitler.

In 1933 Germany's first concentration camp, Dachau, was opened near Munich. It was run by Hitler's *Schutzstaffeln*, an elite protection and security service, known as the SS. Once confined behind the camp's barbed wire, "critics" of the regime—both Jewish and non-Jewish—received brutal and savage treatment. At Dachau the pattern was set for the operation of the dozens of concentration and extermination camps to which prisoners from all over Europe were to be sent in the near future.

"Even though we could see what was coming," Mama recalled sadly, "we hung on for the sake of our elderly parents. But many Jews were already leaving Germany."

Indeed, by the end of 1937 about 130,000, a quarter of Germany's Jews, had emigrated. Many made their way to Holland,

Belgium, Switzerland, France, England, or the Americas. Some managed to enter Palestine, while others even relocated in the distant city of Shanghai in China. The United States was the most favored destination. But documents for that country were the most difficult to obtain because its immigration quota was very limited.

Leaving Germany was both painful and costly. Family and friends remained behind. Jewish properties and businesses had to be sold to Germans for far less than their true market values. And the German government demanded compensation for the privilege of emigration.

"But all this," Mama said, "we would have done. Except that now Oma, in her seventies, was ill with cancer."

Then, early in 1938, the picture changed drastically for the younger Blumenthals. Oma, Marion's grandmother, aged seventy-two, died. And within weeks her death was followed by that of Opa, aged eighty-three, who suffered a heart attack. Although deeply saddened, the family agreed that the deaths of Oma and Opa had spared them the difficulty of being forcibly removed from their lifelong home.

Now there was no more time to be lost. Four months after Opa's death the store and its contents, the building, and most of the Blumenthals' household goods were sold, for a fraction of their worth. In the spring of 1938 Ruth and Walter, five-year-old Albert, and three-year-old Marion left the small town of Hoya and moved into an apartment in the city of Hanover.

"Why did we go to Hanover? For one purpose," Mama explained. "To work on getting papers for the United States and to leave for there as soon as possible."

"Soon," however, did not mean within a couple of months. Ruth and Walter knew all too well that the process could be painfully slow, taking as long as two years.

The United States, once a haven for immigrants, had tightened its admissions policy during the 1920s and had kept its doors virtually shut through the depression of the 1930s. In 1938 it planned to admit only about 27,000 immigrants from Germany *and* Austria.

On March 12, 1938, Hitler had annexed Austria, Germany's neighbor and the country of his birth. Pro-Nazi sentiments ran high in Austria, and Austrian Jews immediately began to look for a means of escape, increasing the demand for places on the U.S. quota list. Yet, on the basis of recent practice, it seemed all too likely that the U.S. immigration authorities would issue even *fewer* quota numbers than the 27,000 that had been allotted for the year.

In addition to getting on the quota list, a foreigner needed an affidavit—a written guarantee from a relative, a friend, or some other acceptable sponsor already living in the United States—that the newcomer would be cared for financially and would not become a public charge.

Lastly, the would-be immigrant had to obtain a visa. This all-important document was the actual permission to enter the United States. Often the visa was stamped directly into the person's passport, another document that had to be in perfect order.

"We already had the affidavit," Mama said. "It was from Tante [Aunt] Clara, a sister of Walter's who lived in New York City. So you can imagine our joy when we were notified in Hanover that on September thirteenth, 1938, we had been placed on the quota list for the United States!"

There, indeed, was the official notice, with the four quota numbers running in sequence from 7375 to 7378, one for each member of the Blumenthal family. Now all that was lacking was the visa.

How soon would it come through? With luck it might be issued within a year. But it would be a dangerous year. For Hitler not only was closing in steadily on the Jews but also appeared to be pushing Germany toward a massive takeover of Europe. Was there enough time left in which to escape Hitler's grasp and move on to a new life in America?

CHAPTER 3

"Get Dressed and Come with Us"

In the Blumenthal apartment in Hanover the children lay ill with whooping cough. Although the most serious stage of the disease had passed, Marion and Albert still coughed and made frightening gagging sounds in the night. Ruth and Walter rose frequently to comfort them.

It was now November 1938, and the bleak German autumn had begun. It was much too soon to expect news of the visa that would take the family to America. "Patience . . . we must have patience," the worried parents told themselves.

But the autumn of 1938 was a frightening time to be waiting

for a way out of Germany. During the summer organized gangs of Nazis had set fire to and destroyed the main synagogues of Nuremberg and Munich, another important city of southern Germany.

The government claimed that such acts were merely "random" violence against Jews. But at the same time Hitler was introducing new measures to identify Germany's Jews and to isolate them from the rest of society. On August 17 a law was passed that forced all Jewish females to take the middle name Sarah. All males were to be given the name Israel, and these names were to be added to existing legal documents, such as birth certificates, marriage certificates, and passports. Not long afterward, on October 5, it was decreed that all passports and other documents held by Germany's Jews must also be marked with a large letter *J*.

During the six months the Blumenthals lived in Hanover, they made few friends. "We hoped, of course," Mama said, "that we would be there only a short time. But we were lucky in our good Jewish neighbors, the Dannenbergs, who also turned out to be our very good friends."

The Dannenberg family—Bertha, Walter, and their son, Gerd, or Gary, who was two years older than Albert—lived on the floor above the Blumenthals in the small Hanover apartment building.

"On the eighth of November," Mama recalled, "Mr. Dannenberg visited us with a warning. There was going to be 'some trouble.' It had to do with the Polish Jews who were being deported from Germany."

The expulsion of thousands of Jews who had been in Polish territory but had lived in Germany since 1918 was another of Hitler's measures to make Germany racially pure. The roundup of this group had begun on October 28. Swiftly and brutally some 18,000 Polish-born Jews were torn from their homes and businesses, packed into trains, and dumped just short of the Polish border. There they were stripped of all their belongings except ten marks and forced to walk the rest of the way into Poland.

Many lived in the stables and pigsties of farms on the Polish frontier until they could find relatives or friends to take them in. One deportee, Zindel Grynszpan, managed to send a postcard to his son, seventeen-year-old Herschel, who had earlier fled to Paris. Infuriated, the young man bought a pistol, entered the German Embassy in Paris, and shot the first official he met, Ernst vom Rath, a third secretary to the ambassador. The date was November 7, 1938.

As vom Rath lay seriously wounded, a growing fear gripped the Jewish people of Germany. Suppose vom Rath died, the victim of a Jewish assassin. Hitler would surely exact a violent revenge, especially at a time so close to the notorious Nazi memorial date of November 9.

It was on November 9, 1923, that Hitler had been arrested in Munich for his unsuccessful attempt—known as the Beer Hall Putsch—to overthrow the German government. Ever since the Nazis had come to power in 1933, November 9 was the day on which the party celebrated its triumph. Hitler went back to Munich to meet with his old guard, massive rallies were held, and promotions were made within the party ranks.

"Guns," Mr. Dannenberg warned the Blumenthals when he visited them on the evening of November 8. "If you have a gun in the house, get rid of it. If they make a search and they find it, you will be finished."

It had been illegal for some time for a Jew to own a firearm of any sort. But Walter was still in possession of his service revolver. He was proud of his record during the war of 1914–1918 and thought of himself as a loyal member of the German Army. Even though the Nazis had taken over in Germany, it seemed impossible that he could be arrested, even sentenced to death, for having kept the revolver he'd owned while defending the country.

Yet both he and Ruth knew that this was true. "So, on that very evening," Mama said, "we took the revolver and wrapped it in many layers of paper. Then, very late, we went out and walked to a nearby park where there was an artificial lake. We were very careful that nobody saw us. Then we silently dropped Walter's service revolver into the lake and came home."

The next day, November 9, vom Rath died in Paris. All that day things were strangely quiet in Germany. Hitler was in Munich for his political victory celebration. Many people expected he would make a frenzied speech on the radio, calling for severe new anti-Jewish measures. But evening came, it grew late, and people began to prepare for bed. In the Blumenthal apartment all was still except for the spasms of coughing from the sick children.

Then, an hour or so after midnight, Nazi marching songs and the sharp rhythm of hobnailed boots began to be heard in the streets of Hanover. These were followed by sounds of shouting, the crack of pistol shots, and what seemed to be the crashing of broken glass. Occasionally, too, the sky flickered with tongues of orange light from distant fires.

The sounds of terror rose and fell, well into the small hours of the morning of November 10, as the rampaging storm troops drew closer to the Blumenthal building, only to retreat in some other direction. Then, sometime between 4:00 and 5:00 A.M., there was an explosion that rocked the entire city. Nazi demolition teams had blown up the Central Synagogue, a thick-walled building that was one of the largest religious structures in Hanover.

In the Blumenthal apartment, and even at a much greater distance from the synagogue, the windows rattled violently. "It was soon afterward, sometime around five A.M.," Mama related, "that we heard the thud of rifle butts at the downstairs entrance to the building." A few moments later the bell rang and there was a sharp rapping at the door of the Blumenthals' second-floor apartment.

"It was the Gestapo, the secret state police," Mama said. "They asked for Papa by name. 'Get dressed,' they said, 'and come with us.' Just like that. 'Get dressed and come with us.'

"While Walter was hastily putting on his clothes, they searched the apartment. At that time the Nazis were taking away only men, not women or children. How fortunate, though, that we had gotten rid of the gun.

"When Walter was fully dressed and ready to go, he asked the officers, 'May I go to the synagogue first to say my morning prayers?' 'No!' they replied angrily. They had searched the apartment but had found nothing of value. 'That car out front,' one of them asked. 'Is it yours?' 'Yes,' Walter answered. 'Give us the keys,' the officer demanded. Walter handed them over, and of course, we never saw the car again. But that was the least of it. The question was, Where were they taking Papa? Would we ever see him again?"

All over Germany and Austria the outburst of violence against the Jews continued throughout November 10. In Hanover, which had been Herschel Grynszpan's hometown, scattered acts of vengeance continued even longer. Gradually the extent of the damage was learned.

In Germany alone, some eight thousand Jewish-owned shops had had their windows smashed and their contents looted. Two hundred synagogues had been destroyed, their Torah scrolls and holy books burned. Unoccupied Jewish houses and apartments had been entered by force. Furniture and even pianos were heaved from balconies into the streets below. Possessions of every sort crackled in the bonfires that leaped up on numerous street corners. But it was the vast amount of shattered glass that gave the infamous night of November 9–10 the name of *Kristallnacht*, Night of Broken Glass.

The human toll was the largest to date. Ninety-one Jews were known to have died in the street violence alone, and more than thirty thousand Jewish men were taken away to concentration camps. Since Germany's Jewish population had declined from 500,000 to 300,000 by late 1938, the prisoners represented one of every ten Jews.

Many men from the Hanover area were taken to Buchenwald. This camp, near Weimar, to the southeast of Hanover, had been patterned after Dachau. It was run by the SS and was used as a concentration and forced-labor camp for political and racial prisoners. Those arrested were taken by truck to the railroad station, transported by train to Weimar, and then by truck to the camp itself.

Was Buchenwald where Papa had been taken? Mr. Dannenberg, who had gone into hiding during *Kristallnacht* and had escaped arrest, had now returned home. He suspected Walter was at Buchenwald. But wherever Walter had been taken, it was important that Ruth go immediately to Gestapo headquarters in Hanover and present the document of September 13, 1938, from the American Consulate in Hamburg, stating that the Blumenthal family had been placed on the quota list for immigration into the United States.

"This good advice," Mama said, "I took at once. Although I hated to go near the Gestapo, I did what Mr. Dannenberg suggested."

At the office of the Gestapo, Ruth found a waiting room filled with women seeking information about their husbands, sons, and fathers. In contrast with the chaos and brutality of a few days earlier, there was amazing order and even civility at the police headquarters. People were called in one by one, and those, like Ruth, who had valid papers proving their family's intention to emigrate, were told that their loved ones would be released shortly.

As the days passed and there was no sign of Walter, Ruth began to go each evening to the Hanover railway station to meet the incoming train from Weimar. Some of those arrested on *Kristallnacht* returned, but Walter was not among them. And each day the news of what went on at Buchenwald grew worse. It was reported that new arrivals were made to stand at attention for hours. The slightest movement could mean a blow with rifle butt or even a prolonged beating. The men slept in narrow barrack bunks atop one another, and were given little food or water. Some were put to work in a nearby stone quarry. It was shattering for Ruth to think of Walter, always dignified and deeply proud of his ability to protect his family, so helpless and degraded.

When her spirits were at their lowest, a postcard arrived from Walter. It was dated November 18, and it was indeed from Buchenwald. A printed notice on the card warned the prisoner to use a large, clear handwriting, or the censors would not pass it on for delivery.

"My loved ones," Walter had written, "I am, thank God, healthy and hope the same of you. Don't write to me because there is no incoming mail. . . . Don't send money. Hope our two darlings are well again. Hugs and kisses to you all. Walter, Papa."

He had written nothing about when he would be released. Had the Gestapo officer broken his promise to forward notice of Walter's status as the holder of an American quota number to the camp? What should Ruth do? That night and the next she went again to the railroad station in vain. On the night of the twenty-first she remained at home.

Very late that evening the doorbell rang. Fearful of bad news, Ruth went to the door. It was Walter, wearing the same clothes in which he'd been arrested, now dirty and rumpled. He had not been able to bathe or shave during the eleven days he'd spent in the camp. Not that evening or at any future time did he speak of what his life in Buchenwald had been like. The only thing he told Ruth and the children was that before being discharged, he had been required to sign a document stating that he had been "correctly treated." Also, according to the terms of his release, he and his family were to be out of Germany within three months.

"Who," Ruth asked, "would *want* to stay in Germany after *Kristallnacht*? It was more than just a warning. It was the beginning of the end."

Now, indeed, it was clear that not only would Jews who remained on German soil live as impoverished and despised outcasts, but their very survival from day to day would be in question. Nor did it appear that any other nation was going to interfere in Germany's internal affairs, least of all in its treatment of Jews.

On November 12, as an immediate aftermath of *Kristallnacht*, the government levied a fine of one billion marks on its Jewish population for the damage caused by the Jewish presence in the country. The real purpose of this enormous "expiation payment" was to make sure that no Jew profited from an insurance claim for destroyed property and to drain off as much as possible of any remaining Jewish wealth. This money and similar levies were to help Germany rearm itself for the war it was planning to wage for the conquest of Europe.

The Blumenthal apartment in Hanover was now the scene of urgent preparations for departure. "We were lucky," Ruth said, "to get a permit to leave for Holland, where Tante Rosi, Walter's youngest sister, who had married a Dutch citizen, lived. Not everybody could get a permit just to pick up and go to another country."

By late December the family's furniture and other possessions that had been brought from Hoya were ready to be packed into three large containers. These were to go into storage in the Dutch port city of Rotterdam, for it was from there that the Blumenthals planned to sail to the United States. Meantime, they would wait in Holland for the still-lacking visa.

Included in the containers were linens and silver that would one day be part of four-year-old Marion's wedding trousseau. Handing down such items was a family tradition that went back for generations.

For the train journey to Holland the Blumenthals would carry only a few suitcases. However, before their packing could be completed, all the goods they were taking out of Germany had to be inspected by the *Zollfahndungs Stelle,* a special customs agency set up to confiscate jewelry, gold watches, silverware, and other items of value.

"But," said Mama, "when they came to the apartment, they went much further than just taking jewelry. Of the twelve blankets we owned, they allowed us to keep only four. Of warm coats, only one for each of us. For jewelry, they allowed me only a watch and my wedding band. Then they wrapped everything they were taking away from us in the blankets, slung them over their shoulders, and left. They didn't even give us a receipt."

In January 1939, carrying only the small departure allowance of ten marks in cash, Ruth and Walter, four-year-old Marion, and six-year-old Albert boarded the train for Holland. Their neighbors the Dannenbergs bade them farewell and promised to see that the three containers of household goods remaining in the apartment in Hanover would be picked up and transported to Rotterdam.

"Even though it meant leaving behind almost everything

we had worked so hard for," Mama said, "we were relieved and glad to put dangerous Germany behind us. We hoped we would be safe, at least until the time came for us to sail for the United States. Yet in our hearts we sensed that this was going to be the start of an uneasy and worrisome life—and, yes, an uncertain future."

Hitler, the Nazi party leader, delivering a speech in 1935, one year after he had become both chancellor and president of Germany

Followers of Hitler offering the Nazi salute at a rally in Berlin, the German capital

The yellow Star of David with the word "Jude" (German for "Jew") inscribed in black

Members of the Hitler Youth in uniform; the swastika armband was worn on the left arm

Brown-shirted Nazi storm troopers enforcing the 1933 boycott of Jewish-owned businesses; the sign reads: GERMANS! DEFEND YOURSELVES! DON'T BUY FROM JEWS!

The Blumenthal family's house
and store in Hoya, Germany,
in 1930

Ruth Moses and Walter Blumenthal
visiting Hanover during their engagement,
August 1931

In Hoya, 1935:
Ruth with Marion,
six months old,
and Albert, age
two and a half

Albert and Marion,
ages five and three,
after the family's
move from Hoya
to Hanover

The Central Synagogue of
Hanover after it was blown up
by Nazi demolition teams on
Kristallnacht in November 1938

Walter Blumenthal's postcard, written to his family from Buchenwald on November 18, 1938, stating that he is well but telling them not to write, inquire after him, or send money

Konzentrationslager Buchenwald
Kommandantur

Weimar-Buchenwald, den 21. November 19 38.

Entlassungsschein

Der Schutzhäftling ~~Vorbeugungshäftling~~ Walter Blumenthal

geb. am 19.11.96 in Hoxa hat vom 11.11.38

bis zum heutigen Tage im Konzentrationslager Buchenwald eingesessen.

Auf Anordnung des Stapoleit Hannover ~~Geheimen Staatspolizeiamtes Berlin~~ ~~Reichskriminalpolizeiamtes Berlin~~ vom 17.11.38

wurde er nach Hannover entlassen.

Der Lagerkommandant

SS-Standartenführer

Kö.-

Discharge certificate from Buchenwald concentration camp; after eleven days of imprisonment, Walter Blumenthal is ordered to report immediately to the Hanover State Police

Westerbork in the Netherlands, at first a refugee camp and later a transit camp, encircled by a moat dug by Jewish prisoners

Ruth, Marion,
Walter, and Albert
in Westerbork in
May 1941, one year
after their hopes of
emigrating to the
United States had
vanished

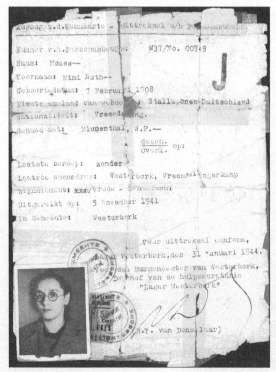

Auszug a.d. Kennkarte – Uittreksel u/h persoonsbewijs

Nummer v.h. Persoonsbewijs: W37/No. 00749

Naam: Moses—

Voornaam: Mimi Ruth—

Geboortedatum: 7 Februari 1908

Plaats en land van geboorte: Stallupönen-Duitschland

Nationaliteit: Vreemdeling.

Gehuwd met: Blumenthal, W.P.—

Gesch.
Overl. op:

Laatste beroep: zonder

Laatste woonadres: Westerbork, Vreemdelingenkamp

Rijksinkomst: xxxx Vrouw L Winterhulp

Uitgereikt op: 5 November 1941

In Gemeente: Westerbork

Voor uittreksel conform,

Westerbork, den 31 Januari 1944,

Voor den Burgemeester van Westerbork,
De Chef van de hulpsecretarie
"Lager Westerbork"

(A.T. van Donselaar)

Ruth Blumenthal's
work identification card,
issued in Westerbork
November 5, 1941; the
letter J indicates that
the cardholder is Jewish

A transport list of those Westerbork prisoners being shipped to Bergen-Belsen in February 1944; the four members of the Blumenthal family are designated as "stateless," and Marion's name appears as the sometimes-used "Leonie"

No:	Name:	Vorname:	Geburts- datum:	Nationalität:
251	Bierman-Cohen	Ruth	24.1.23	Holl.
252	Biermann	Salomon	15.12.00	Engl./Holl.
253	Bigielman	Albert	1.11.32	Franz.
254	Bigielman-Rachman	Fajga	14.11.96	Poln.
255	Bimbad	Denise	9.2.36	Franz.
256	Bimbad-Safro	Lea	11.8.05	Litauen
257	Bimbad	Madeleine	14.6.30	Franz.
258	Bing	Felix	7.10.10	Ecuador
259	Bing-Schotter	Franciska	15.3.08	
260	Birenhak-Hauser	Oila	20.4.14	Paraguay
261	Birenhak	Koppel	29.10.01	
262	Birenhak	Moses	4.11.12	
263	Birenhak-Keller	Perla	23.10.13	
264	Birenhak-Wald	Rachela	1.4.72	
265	Birnbaum-Szaja	Hene	29.6.05	Staatl.
266	Birnbaum	Jacob	14.12.31	
267	Birnbaum	Julius	21.9.21	Holl.
268	Birnbaum	Osiasz	5.11.02	Staatl.
269	Birnbaum	Regina	7.9.30	
270	Birnbaum	Samuel	26.12.58	
271	Birnbaum	Sonnie	26.5.28	
272	Birnbaum	Susahne	31.7.34	
273	Birnbaum	Therese	29.12.88	Holl.
274	Birnbaum	Zwi	10.4.33	Staatl.
275	Blech	Sally	2.6.80	
276	Bies	Jeanne	21.5.75	Holl.
277	Blik	Clara	14.2.37	Holl./Engl.
278	Blik-Samson	Marie	19.9.10	
279	Bill	Moritz	21.4.39	
280	Blitz	Bernard	30.8.27	Holl.
281	Blitz-Davids	Helene	31.1.01	
282	Blitz	Martijn	18.5.97	
283	Blitz	Nanette	6.4.29	
284	Blitz-Nabarro	Schoontje	8.3.81	
285	Bloch	Andries	28.7.95	Paraguay
286	Bloch-Elte	Gesina	4.6.01	
287	Bloch	Mayer	4.5.32	
288	Bloch	Olga	30.8.00	Staatl.
289	Bloch-Dreyfus	Renee	9.4.11	Franz.
290	Blok,gesch.Cohn	Grete	14.10.99	Holl.
291	Blok,Jesman	Charlotte	13.4.20	Engl./Holl.
292	Blokjesman	Jacques	28.12.21	
293	Blumenstein	Joseph	1.3.78	Staatl.
294	Blumenstein-Jacobsohn	Kate	22.8.96	
295	Blumenstein	Lonny	28.6.32	
296	Blumenthal	Albert	11.10.32	
297	Blumenthal	Leonie	20.12.34	
298	Blumenthal-Moses	Ruth	7.2.08	
299	Blumenthal	Walter	19.11.97	
300	Boas	Elias	26.1.40	Holl.

Men, women, and children from Westerbork transit camp waiting to board a deportation train bound for one of the concentration camps in Germany or eastern Europe

CHAPTER 4

"Escape to Holland"

On arriving in Rotterdam, the Blumenthals began at once to experience the difficulties of living as exiles. About 20,000 German Jews had already fled to the Netherlands, a country that had long been tolerant of Jews and that had a Jewish population of its own of roughly 118,000.

Some German refugees who had left Germany in the early thirties had been able to transfer their businesses to Holland and to establish comfortable lives for their families. But no such opportunities existed for those Jews who arrived in the later 1930s, stripped of their possessions and essentially homeless.

"At first," Mama said, "we were shifted around from one refugee center to another. All of them were overcrowded and had separate sleeping quarters for men, women, and children. Marion was frightened of sleeping with so many strange children, and she cried all the time.

"After three months we were given the opportunity to move to another place in Holland, Gouda, where there was a camp for Jewish refugee children, ages eight to fifteen. They had been sent there for safety from other parts of Nazi-dominated Europe.

"The work," Ruth recalled, "was very hard, cooking, serving meals, and caring for the children—a hundred twenty-five or so, some of whom were orphans. But at least we could live there as a family during that summer of 1939, and Marion was no longer afraid."

While the Blumenthals tried to make the best of their life in Holland, deeply threatening events were taking place elsewhere in Europe. In keeping with his plans to expand Germany's territory eastward, Hitler had attacked and occupied Czechoslovakia on March 15, 1939. When this bold move met with no opposition from other nations, he went ahead with his next conquest, Poland, on September 1, 1939. Two days later

Great Britain and France declared war on Germany and the conflict that became known as World War II began.

How long, people in the Netherlands wondered, would the Nazis respect Dutch neutrality? Especially at risk were the nation's Jews, who, including refugees from nations other than Germany, now totaled about 140,000. And most immediate was the problem of how to accommodate the jobless Jewish refugees who continued to pour into the country.

In the fall of 1939, with contributions from Holland's Committee for Special Jewish Affairs, the Dutch government set up a permanent refugee camp in northeastern Holland to be known as Westerbork. The camp was located on a desolate and windswept moor, bitterly cold in winter and plagued with heat, flies, and sandstorms in summer. But it offered a home of sorts for Holland's Jewish refugees.

On October 9, 1939, the first twenty-two families moved in. Each was given a small, self-contained unit in which to live. When the Blumenthals arrived at Westerbork a couple of months later, they, too, were assigned to one of the two hundred or so "little houses." Actually these units were connected to one another in rows, having the outward appearance of ordinary barracks. But they did have the advantage of being centrally heated.

"It was not so bad at all," Ruth said. "We had a small kitchen, with a sink and a hot plate that had one burner. This was just for coffee, tea, snacks, and so forth. All our regular meals we ate in a communal dining hall.

"We also had a bathroom with a toilet and a sink. There was no tub or shower, so we could take only sponge baths. But there was also a bathhouse in the camp.

"In the largest room of the four, we had a table and chairs and a bed that folded up against the wall during the day. This was where Walter and I slept. Marion and Albert slept in a smaller room just behind ours, in double-decker bunk beds."

Like the rest of the new residents, Ruth and Walter were assigned to work details from 7:00 A.M. to noon and from 2:00 P.M. to 7:00 in the evening. Ruth was given a job in the kitchen, where the food for the communal dining room was prepared. Walter worked in the shoe repair shop. There was even some makeshift schooling for the children. These activities helped pass the days as the family continued to wait for the longed-for visa for America.

"We worried," Ruth said, "about all the changes of address we'd had since moving from Hanover, so we left a careful trail behind us. We were ready to pick ourselves up at a moment's notice, for even before leaving Germany, we had paid our passage to America on the Dutch ship *Nieuw Amsterdam*.

"And, at last, in January 1940—after a wait of fifteen months—we received our American visa in the camp at Westerbork. Immediately we booked space for March 1940, the first available sailing out of Rotterdam. Two more months in Holland, and we would be on our way!"

While Ruth and Walter made plans for the family's departure for Europe, Marion and Albert fell into the rhythm of life in their new surroundings. Marion, just turned five, adjusted easily to Westerbork. She made friends with the children of the other German refugee families in the "little houses." Among the adults, old friends and distant relatives found one another in the camp, and there was frequent visiting back and forth.

"It all seemed quite normal to me," Marion recalled, "for I had little else to compare it to. I could remember nothing of our life in Germany, so I did not miss the material things we had enjoyed there. Besides, no one else in Westerbork had much of value either."

Marion remembered her favorite games and pastimes: jump rope, hopscotch, marbles. "One of our hobbies was to collect foil wrappings. My friends and I traded them. The colorful ones were the most valuable. We smoothed them out with our nails and kept them between the pages of a notebook.

"There was another game that I made up to pass the time when I was alone. I would take a small mirror or a piece of glass and go for a walk through the rutted lanes of the camp. The mirror would pick up the reflection of the sun, throwing a little square of light on the ground. I would pretend that this dancing patch of light was my own little puppy on a leash."

In those early months at Westerbork, with only about seven hundred refugees in the camp, the food was plain but plentiful. Pea soup, potatoes, and cabbage dishes were the mainstay. Eggs, meat, and dried fruit were also still available. Marion was especially fond of melted cheese on bread. But what she longed for most were sweets.

"I remember how greedy I was for anything sweet, so much so that I would even eat saccharin tablets. And how I always wanted the bigger share of everything, even though I knew I was supposed to give half to Albert. Papa was very strict about these things and always stressed good manners and politeness. Once when I was given a special treat by one of our neighbors, Papa sensed correctly that I had not said 'thank you.' He made me return at once and say the proper words to express my appreciation."

Spring was now approaching, and the refugees were pleasantly surprised to find yellow- and purple-flowered lupines and carpets of purple heather blooming on the barren heath, almost in their doorways. But Ruth and Walter were not cheered by this sight. There had been bad news concerning their March booking on the *Nieuw Amsterdam*. Because of the huge demand for passage out of Europe, their sailing had been postponed to June 1940.

Meantime, there were growing worries about Germany's plans for further conquest. It soon became clear that Hitler was not going to stop with the occupation of Austria, Czechoslovakia, and Poland. On April 10, 1940, his armies invaded Denmark and Norway.

Which country would be next? The refugees, who had thought themselves safe in the nations that lay to the west of Germany, did not have long to wait for the answer.

On May 10, 1940, Germany invaded Holland, Belgium, Luxembourg, and France. On May 14, the Luftwaffe bombed Rotterdam, Holland's second-largest city and one of the world's biggest seaports. This act of destruction brought about a rapid surrender. Within days the Dutch royal family fled to England and the Nazi occupation of the Netherlands began.

In the badly damaged city of Rotterdam the warehouse in which the Blumenthals' possessions had been stored was reduced to smoking debris. "But," Ruth said, "that was the least of it. We could see now that our escape to Holland had not been an escape at all. Instead we had been caught in a trap."

Ruth was right. There would be no more ocean liners taking refugees to America from the crippled port of Rotterdam. The family would remain in Westerbork, uncertain of its fate under the Nazi regime that had now taken over in the Netherlands.

At first the changes in Westerbork were not as alarming as feared. Additional housing was erected in the form of long wooden barracks, each designed to shelter about three hundred men, women, and children. The barracks had tiers of bunk beds and separate latrines for men and women. Later, as the camp became more crowded, up to six hundred people were forced to occupy a single barrack. But the Blumenthals, like other early residents, remained in their own family unit among the "little houses" in the older part of the camp.

As they had in Germany in the 1930s, the Nazis now began a program designed to impoverish and isolate the Jews of the Netherlands. In October 1940 all Jewish owners of businesses were required to register with the occupation forces. This was the first step in denying Jews employment and stripping them of any means of livelihood.

The following year Holland's Jews had their properties confiscated, their children were forbidden to attend any but Jewish-run schools, and curfews and other restrictions on their movements were imposed.

In May 1942, to help enforce the many anti-Jewish decrees, all Jews residing in Holland were ordered to sew the yellow star onto their outer garments. The center of the six-pointed star bore the black-lettered word *Jood*—Dutch for "Jew"—instead of the German *Jude*. In Germany the wearing of the star had begun in September 1941.

In July 1942 German Jewish boys and girls, ages fifteen to eighteen, living in the Netherlands began to receive call-up notices. They were to report without delay to "work camps" in eastern Europe. It was at this point that many Jews, both Dutch and German, went into hiding.

At Westerbork the big change took place on July 1, 1942,

when the Germans officially took over command from the Dutch. Immediately watchtowers were built and a barbed-wire fence was put up around the entire camp. Also, daily roll calls began. But most ominous was the change in the camp's name. What had been known simply as the Central Camp for Refugees, Westerbork, was renamed, under German command, Police-Supervised Transit Camp, Westerbork.

The word *transit* held the key to Westerbork's future as a feeder camp. For the next two years and some months, Westerbork served as a deportation center from which more than 100,000 Jews were shipped from Holland to Germany's most notorious concentration camps. At least 60,000 were sent to Auschwitz, in Poland. There most met deaths in the gas chambers. Their bodies were then burned in the crematorium ovens. The Germans boasted that at the peak of its killing activity in 1943 and 1944 the extermination camp known as Auschwitz-Birkenau could dispose of as many as 4,756 bodies every twenty-four hours.

"What did we know of Auschwitz," Ruth said, "in that summer of 1942? We knew, and we didn't know. Some people, especially the younger ones, believed that being 'resettled' in the East meant they were going to be put to work in German war factories. That didn't seem so bad to them. But there were rumors of much worse things. For most of us, I guess, the truth was that we didn't *want* to know."

As the Blumenthals suspected, there *were* worse things. By June 1942 reports of Jews' being gassed in Poland had already appeared in American and British newspapers and been aired on the BBC. But the horrifying accounts of the slaughter of 700,000 Polish Jews were so monstrous that most of the world refused to believe them.

On July 15, 1942, the first of the ninety-three transports left Westerbork for the East. And almost every week thereafter, sometimes twice a week, a long train of empty cattle cars pulled into the camp siding to take on its human cargo. Most transports averaged a thousand people. But some were as large as three thousand. Men, women, and children, of all ages—some brought on stretchers from the Westerbork camp hospital—were crammed with their belongings into the bare wooden carriages, each carriage provided only with an empty bucket and a pail for sand for toilet functions.

"The street alongside the railway platform," Ruth recalled, "was the only paved road in Westerbork. It was called the Boulevard des Misères, the 'boulevard of misery.' Another name for it was Rachmones Allee or Tsorres Allee, meaning 'street of pity' or 'street of woe.' We were forbidden by the commandant to watch the transports leaving on those terrible mornings. Some people disobeyed and managed to get a glimpse of the long lines of deportees climbing into the cattle cars. But we never did. At other times, when there was no train waiting there, people strolled on the boulevard."

As the months went by, Westerbork grew more and more crowded. Dutch Jews from all over Holland were rounded up by the thousands and brought in to be processed. Some stayed only a few days; others remained for months. None had any control over his or her fate. Even the sick and dying were given only a few hours to ready themselves for the journey.

The Blumenthals now had to share their quarters with another family, a couple called the Hamburgers. Mr. and Mrs. Hamburger took over the smaller room with the bunk beds, and Marion and Albert moved into their parents' room.

"I remember the Hamburgers," Marion said, "because I loved to sing. But Mrs. Hamburger, a tall woman with black hair, whose first name was Hanna, begged me not to because I couldn't carry a tune. She would bribe me by telling me stories. So that wasn't so bad after all. And we were still much better off than the people in the big barracks, so crowded there was hardly room to breathe."

It was now a little more than a year since the Germans had turned Westerbork into a transit camp. Each week the train continued to roll in, and each week the quota of deportees that the Germans demanded had to be filled. As Ruth put it, "We knew that our time was coming."

From the very beginning Walter had been trying to find a way to save his family from Auschwitz. Like the other Westerbork inmates, he explored various means of avoiding deportation to the death camp. One possibility that emerged in mid-1943 was to apply to go to Palestine as an "exchange Jew." The British, who then held Palestine, were not permitting Jews to immigrate freely. But with proper eligibility, Jews living under the Nazis might be exchanged for German prisoners of war captured by Britain and its allies, on a one-to-one basis.

"We believed we *could* be eligible to go to Palestine," Ruth said, "because we had relatives there. My sister Ulla had emigrated to Palestine in 1936 as a *halutza*, a pioneer. So, on August twenty-sixth, 1943, Walter applied through the International Red Cross for an exchange permit that would allow us to go to the camp in Celle, Germany, where the exchanges were arranged. We knew very little about this place, only that there was a special privileged section for those waiting to go to Palestine. We also knew that it was not a camp like Auschwitz, for it had no gas chambers.

"When, on January thirtieth, 1944, we received permission to leave Westerbork for Celle, we were almost joyful. We expected to be in the new camp only a short time before taking the ship for Palestine. The children were especially happy to be going to a new place. Marion was nine years old, and Albert was eleven. They were very bored and were not getting any proper schooling.

"So we set about packing our things. Each of us was allowed to take one knapsack filled with as much as we could stuff into it. Mine contained the old family portraits, letters, and receipts that I had been keeping with me since our arrival in Holland. Our transport to Celle took place on a Tuesday morning in February 1944. We left our quarters in Westerbork, where we had lived for four years, and walked to the Boulevard des Misères, where the train was waiting. There had been so many sad departures from that place, but for us—on our way to Palestine and freedom—we thought it would be different."

CHAPTER 5

"The Greatest Disappointment"

As the Blumenthals approached the Westerbork railroad station, they began to have feelings of uneasiness. They had heard that exchange Jews going to Celle would not be riding in cattle cars. And it was true that there were many third-class carriages attached to the train. These carriages had rows of bench seats inside and windows instead of horizontal wooden slats through which to look out. But the transport was huge.

Nearly a thousand people stood ready to board the twenty or more cars that waited alongside the platform. As always, the uniformed camp police, the camp commandant, and his officers were on the platform, closely monitoring the operation. And once inside the carriages, the Blumenthals and their fellow travelers were packed in as tightly as in any cattle car.

The carriages with seats were, in fact, more uncomfortable and more lacking in privacy than the freight cars, which had no interior fittings at all. The Blumenthals' forebodings now turned into a deep suspicion that there was nothing in the least "special" or "privileged" about being transported to Celle. Nor could they fight back the sickening thought that they were being returned to Germany, from which they had fled five years earlier, this time as prisoners.

With a blast of the whistle the train at last announced its departure. At the camp boundary it stopped once again for a final count of the passengers by the German occupation forces. The total had to be exactly the same as that vouched for by the Westerbork camp commandant. Then, with additional military officers on board to accompany the travelers, the train headed east toward Germany.

The camp to which the Blumenthals were going lay a short distance northwest of Celle, near the small town of Bergen and the village of Belsen, and so it had been named Bergen–Belsen. The journey took about five hours. Although Marion had no idea of its length, she vividly remembered her arrival at the camp itself.

"It was dark, bitterly cold, and raining," Marion recalled. "All I could see, as I stepped down onto the ground, were the tall, shiny black boots of the SS officers and their dogs—huge, restless, and mean-looking. I was nine years old and small for my age. The jaws and fanged teeth of the barking and leaping police dogs were exactly at my eye level. Albert stayed close to me, protective as always, but I cringed. I was very, very frightened."

Originally Bergen-Belsen was intended as a prisoner of war camp. But by early 1944 additional sections had been built. They included a camp for Jews with passports from neutral countries such as Spain, Portugal, and Turkey; a camp for Polish Jews, most of whom would soon to be transported to Auschwitz and murdered there; and a camp for exchange Jews like the Blumenthals.

This section was known as the *Sternlager*, the Star Camp. *Star* probably referred to the prisoners' wearing of the yellow star rather than to any "star," or special status. For although prisoners were allowed to wear their own clothing, and male and female family members could meet briefly during the day, the barracks were crude, dark, and crowded, and the SS and their assistants were harsh and bullying.

"Even the very worst conditions at Westerbork," Ruth said, "were a heaven by comparison. For Bergen-Belsen was hell. The only way we managed to survive in those early months of 1944—cold, hungry, and completely degraded—was on hope. We were waiting for the *Austauch*, the exchange of Jews for German prisoners of war, that would take us to Palestine."

In May 1944, three months after the Blumenthals' arrival at Bergen-Belsen, the names of the Jews scheduled for exchange were at last announced.

"We stood," Ruth recalled, "in the *Sternlager* square, listening carefully as the commanding officer began to read off the list. It was arranged alphabetically, starting, of course, with the *A*'s.

"When he began to read the *B*'s, we held our breaths tightly. Before we knew it, however, he had gone on to the *C*'s and *D*'s. There was no 'Blumenthal.'

"Still, knowing we must keep order, we continued to listen. Perhaps there would be some names out of place. Perhaps there would be a few more names after the *Z*'s. Perhaps there would even be a second list.

"With sinking hearts we heard all the names called. No, there was no Blumenthal. I could tell that Walter was going to go up to speak to the officer in charge. He left his place, approached him respectfully, and saluted as in his army days. Then he asked him politely if our name might have been skipped over.

"'No'—the answer came back—'your name is not on the list.'

"Walter held out the certificate from the International Red Cross. 'But all our papers are in order,' he pleaded. 'Can't you look into this?'

"Already Walter had gone too far. The officer lost his patience. Without warning he struck Walter sharply across the neck and back. '*Sau Jude* [pig Jew],' the officer shrieked, 'go back to your place!'"

In that moment all hope died for the Blumenthals. There had been so many disappointments—the failed escape from Germany, the canceled sailing on the *Nieuw Amsterdam*, the horror of being transferred to the concentration camp of Bergen-Belsen. "But this," Ruth said, "this refusal to honor the Palestine certificate, was the greatest disappointment of all."

At a much later date the family learned that of a group of 1,100 Jews who had been sent to Bergen-Belsen for the promised exchange, only 221 ever reached Palestine. The Jews who were chosen left the camp quietly at the end of June 1944, traveled by train to Istanbul, and safely reached Haifa by ship on July 10. For those who remained behind, no further appeals to the Red Cross or to the Bergen-Belsen camp administration had the slightest effect.

"We went on," Marion said, "with our aimless existence. It was now more important than ever for me to search over and over again for my four perfect pebbles. I knew, even then, that in spite of everything, our family *must* survive.

"Mama was lucky to keep her job in the kitchen. The women in the camp begged to work there because of the chance to get extra food. Often they mobbed the soldiers who held them back. The rest of the time these women spent hours talking about food and exchanging recipes.

"Papa had brought cigarettes with him from Westerbork to trade for extra rations of bread. When those were gone, he saved the ones that were given to male prisoners at Bergen-Belsen from time to time. But after some months had passed, no more were given out. So he saved bread from his own ration. I remember our birthday presents to one another. They were a portion of our week's ration of bread.

"One day at *Appell* a young German guard gave my brother an apple. He must have endangered his own life in doing so. Despite the craving for a crunchy, juicy apple, Albert did not keep it for himself. He divided it into an untold number of pieces. This act of kindness by a German solider was like a flicker of light in the darkness and made our bleak existence more bearable, at least for the moment."

One of the most frightening ordeals at Bergen-Belsen was being taken once a month to the showers. By now, the summer of 1944, the gas chambers at Auschwitz had been operating for two and a half years. Rumors had long been circulating that a death camp gas chamber looked almost exactly like an ordinary public shower room.

"Even though we had been told," Marion said, "there were no gas chambers at Bergen-Belsen, how could we ever be sure? We were marched to a special building, just as in Auschwitz, and were made to undress in the presence of the male guards. We folded our clothes neatly, tied our shoes together, and left them outside. Then we were given a piece of soap and pushed inside. The door was slammed shut, and we waited, terrified, to see if water would come out of the overhead nozzles, or—as in Auschwitz—the killing fumes of the gas known as Zyklon B."

The soap that the prisoners at Bergen-Belsen were given before entering the showers did not guarantee their harmlessness.

For it was common practice at Auschwitz to provide soap—and also the promise of hot coffee or warm soup afterward—in order to maintain calm and to deceive those about to be gassed.

The deadly poison the Germans had chosen to use at Auschwitz and other human extermination centers was originally designed for insect and rodent control. Its purpose was to fumigate ships and warehouses and to disinfect clothing. Zyklon (or Cyclon) B, which looked in its solid form like innocent blue crystals, was packed in airtight canisters. When released into the air through the showerlike nozzles of a gas chamber, it turned into a vapor that brought death within fifteen minutes.

After the gas had dissipated, the Auschwitz camp attendants, who were usually prisoners themselves, salvaged the gold from the teeth of the dead, pulled rings from their fingers, and cut off the women's hair. This booty, along with the clothing of the newly dead and the contents of their suitcases, was sent back to Germany, where it had many uses. The corpses of the gassed prisoners were then burned to ash in the Auschwitz ovens.

Bergen-Belsen, too, had a crematorium. Its high, square chimney was similar in appearance to that of Auschwitz. But its chief use was to burn the bodies of those who had died of natural causes—starvation, exhaustion, disease. Later, as the camp filled beyond its capacity, the crematorium could no longer keep up with the body count. The dead at Bergen-Belsen were then burned in open pits, tossed into mass graves, or even strewn about aboveground.

"The stench of burning flesh from those open pits," Marion said, "remains in my nostrils to this day. It was even worse than the foul odors of disease, decay, and lack of sanitation that we drew in with every breath."

Slowly, starting with the Allies' D-day invasion of France in June 1944, the war began to turn against the Germans. At the same time the Russians were gradually closing in from the east. But at Bergen-Belsen, in the autumn of 1944, the worst was yet to come. To hide the evidence of Auschwitz and the other death camps in Poland, the SS now began to drive its prisoners back into the interior of Germany. Bergen-Belsen was to receive an especially large influx.

In the *Sternlager* additional wooden barracks were being built, but they were not ready in time for a transport of more than 3,600 women from Auschwitz-Birkenau. In the cold and wet of autumn the women were crammed into a tent city, with a latrine dug in the mud.

For the Blumenthals and their fellow prisoners, the winter of 1944–1945 proved the most difficult yet. Food had become extremely scarce, and there was no longer enough water for bathing, washing clothes, or even drinking. The cold was intense.

"As I had learned to do the winter before," Marion explained, "I followed the advice of the older women to prevent frostbite of my fingers and toes. After standing at roll call, sometimes for hours, we would return to our barracks and warm our extremities with our own urine.

"Now one of my main occupations was to pick the lice from my clothing one by one and destroy them with my fingernails. Our bodies, our hair, our blankets all were infested, for the barracks themselves were crawling with lice because of the overcrowded and unclean conditions. Hair lice laid their eggs, called nits, in our hair. Clothing lice preferred the seams of our garments and our bedding.

"I remember one garment I loved and tried to preserve. It was an off-white hand-knitted wool cardigan with short sleeves that someone had made for me in Westerbork. Somehow it stretched to fit me as I grew. I still wore it in Bergen-Belsen, for there my body weight was actually decreasing because of the growing hunger."

By the early months of 1945 the food at Bergen-Belsen consisted mainly of cabbage-flavored water and moldy bread. This ration was far less than the six hundred calories a day per inmate that the camp had formerly provided. The prisoners found themselves longing for the turnip soup with bits of gristly horsemeat and the pats of yellow grease called butter that they had received in "better" days.

Despite the total breakdown in the food supply and in sanitary conditions, the SS continued to concentrate on preventing escape. Daily roll call went on for hours in the numbing cold. The police dogs—so dangerous that their handlers had to wear thick armguards and carry dog whips and pistols—continued to terrify the shivering inmates standing at *Appell.*

The death toll was now mounting rapidly as the result of exposure, hunger, severe diarrhea, and fevers. In addition, as the winter drew to an end, the lice-borne disease known as typhus began to spread throughout the camp. Its symptoms were high fever, a red rash, headache, and delirium, often resulting in death. By March 1945, 35,000 out of 60,000 prisoners at Bergen-Belsen had died, mainly of typhus.

"Yes," Marion said, "death had become a moment-to-moment occurrence. In our dark, crowded quarters we often tripped and fell over the newly dead. Their bodies could not be taken away quickly enough.

"Yet even with these terrible sights all around us, even with the stench of the overflowing latrines in our nostrils, those of us who could still function yearned above all for food. Bread came first among our longings, which we called the three B's: bread, bed, and bath. For food was survival.

"One evening in early April 1945 Mama, who still worked in the kitchen, was able to smuggle some potatoes, turnips, and salt into our barrack. She also brought an empty can, and with some splintered wood from our bed slats she managed to build a small fire over which to cook a soup. We had carefully chosen a place on the uppermost 'bed' of a triple-decker bunk where we and some others could shield our illegal and dangerous activity.

"The soup took a long time to cook. It was still bubbling away and was almost done when Mama and I heard the sound of the guards approaching for a surprise visit. I was sitting on the bed near the pot of soup with my right leg bent at the knee. In our haste to cover up what we were doing, we tipped over the pot and the boiling soup spilled across my leg, scalding the lower part from the knee down.

"I was just a few months past my tenth birthday, but I

did not utter a sound. I knew better than to cry out. In our fourteen months in Bergen-Belsen the Nazis had tried to break us physically, spiritually, and emotionally. This forced us to learn self-discipline the hard way. Perhaps it was good that I had always been stubborn and strong-willed. Mama and I lost the soup that evening but not our lives."

Medical treatment of any kind had long ceased to be available at the camp, which was now in a state of almost complete turmoil. The war, it was rumored, would be over soon. Allied bombers roared overhead even during daylight hours, while at night the rumbling of Allied artillery could be heard shelling western front German cities. Would the camp commandant, Josef Kramer, the notorious "Beast of Belsen," surrender the camp peacefully or would he order his SS to attempt a last stand, resulting in mass murder?

For some 8,000 prisoners, the Blumenthals among them, the outcome would remain in question. Within days of the boiling-soup accident that had severely burned Marion's leg, the members of the her family learned that they were to be evacuated "to the East."

"On April ninth, 1945," Marion said, "we were marched to the station and put aboard a long train of cattle cars. My leg was now infected and oozing a thick yellow pus. The pain was very great, and I could not walk. We did not know that Auschwitz had been liberated by the Russians in January 1945, and we were sure that was where the Germans were sending us. It made no sense for them to ship us east when other prisoners were being evacuated to the West. But that was how it appeared, and we were given no explanation of anything.

"Once more, this time so close to the war's end, it seemed that our chances for survival were being snatched away from us and that death loomed closer than ever."

Six days later, on April 15, 1945, British troops reached Bergen-Belsen and liberated the camp. The commandant, Josef Kramer, gave it up without a struggle. He was later tried by a British military court and hanged. The thousands of prisoners who were still alive were freed and cared for. But the Blumenthals were not among them.

CHAPTER 6

"On the Death Train"

"I don't remember," Marion said, "how we covered the distance of three to four miles to the railroad loading platform at the town of Belsen. I am sure that, weak as he was, Papa must have carried me.

"Albert, of course, would have shouldered as many of our belongings as he could, as well as the knapsack in which he always managed to have at least a crust of bread or a raw turnip to share with the rest of us. Mama, too, carried a knapsack with personal belongings and precious documents, receipts, letters, and mementos, including our old family photographs. One good thing about the evacuation from Bergen–Belsen, fright-ening as it was, was that we were allowed to be reunited as a family and to remain that way."

The train that awaited the Blumenthals and their fellow prisoners had recently emptied itself of other prisoners who had been transported *to* Bergen–Belsen from the East. In fact, the ragged, hollow-eyed groups actually passed each other on foot, moving in opposite directions. Later the 2,500 Belsen evacuees learned that they were the last of the three groups to leave the camp. The balance of the 8,000 evacuees had departed earlier, starting on April 6.

The first group had been taken to the concentration camp of Theresienstadt, or Terezin, in Czechoslovakia, which was lib-erated by Soviet Army units on May 8, 1945. The second group had been shunted back and forth across north-central Germany until it was liberated by American troops near Magdeburg, a short distance to the east of Bergen–Belsen. The occupants of the third train were not so fortunate.

"As bad as Bergen–Belsen was," Ruth recalled, "we were terrified to be going on transport to what seemed like almost certain death. Why would the Germans want to empty the *Sternlager* so near to the end of the war? Was it because they had so many exchange Jews in the camp who had never been sent to Palestine? We were the evidence of their broken promises to the International Red Cross. Was that why they wanted to have us destroyed before the Allies arrived and learned the truth?"

As ordered, the prisoners climbed into the boxcars. At first, with only about fifty people to a car, there was room to spread out and arrange themselves in their new quarters. It was agreed that the pail of drinking water and the toilet bucket would be kept as far apart as possible, at diagonally opposite ends of the cars.

The prisoners now waited for the doors to be slid shut and bolted from the outside and for the train to start rolling. But oddly, nothing happened. The day was warm and sunny, and soon some of the bolder evacuees ventured down from the cars. A pile of rotting rutabagas, the turniplike vegetables that made up much of the camp fare, lay near the end of the platform. People began to sort through them for those that were the least odorous. Some even wandered into a nearby stream and began to bathe. Surprisingly the SS guards who were posted around the loading area made no attempt to drive the prisoners back into the cars.

"They didn't even shout a warning," Ruth said. "So why

didn't any of us make a run for it? *We* couldn't because we had a child with a serious leg wound. But some of the others might have made it into the dark pine forest beyond the loading ramp.

"The answer, surely, was that no matter where we hid we would still be surrounded by Nazi Germany. So close to defeat, the country would be more dangerous than ever for an escaped Jewish prisoner. No, there was still no place to run."

All that day the train remained at the siding, its doors wide open. By early evening the prisoners had begun to build fires of dried twigs alongside the railroad track and to cook soups with the half-rotted rutabagas and any other roots or herbs they'd managed to dig up. Then, as darkness fell, they were herded back into the cars. The doors were bolted, and they awaited the start of the journey to an unknown destination.

After a fitful night the prisoners awoke to find themselves still standing at the Bergen railroad siding. The train had not moved. It was now April 10, another pleasant spring day. The routine was much like that of the day before, except that additional prisoners from Bergen-Belsen straggled toward the train and entered the boxcars. Instead of fifty people, each car now held seventy to eighty. Also, bread was distributed to the prisoners, a large chunk that they were told must last them for eight days.

Late that night, its doors again shut and bolted, the train at last began to move.

The next morning, with the train having traveled only about fifteen miles north of Bergen, it halted, and the doors were unbolted. As the SS guards slid them open, they called into each car, *"Toten raus!"* ("Out with the dead!")

Already several cases of typhus had developed on the train, for many of the prisoners had been incubating the disease while still in Bergen-Belsen. The two-week incubation period began with the bite of a louse that carried the typhus germ. No symptoms showed until the deep pink, pea-size spots appeared around the midriff. This rash had given the disease the common name of spotted fever. Its onset was accompanied by a severe headache and a high fever that often resulted in delirious ravings and hallucinations. Death usually followed within one to two days. If, however, the patient survived past the twelfth day, it was believed that there was a good chance for recovery.

"This cry of *'Toten raus!'*," Mama said, "was repeated throughout the trip, as more and more people fell victim to the disease. We prisoners had to bring out our dead. Then the SS would give us pickaxes and shovels to dig a shallow pit alongside the railroad track, while they stood guard over us.

We buried our loved ones, covered over their mass grave, and there we left them.

"One especially pitiful burial was that of a little boy, only seven or eight years old, who was the son of a heavyset Greek Jew named Albala. Albala had been our head Kapo in Bergen-Belsen, and he was hated by all of us. He never failed to give us that extra measure of cruelty when the German command was around to observe him in action. For these cruelties to us, he received special favors and privileges from the Germans.

"But that day, as I watched him place his child's lifeless body alongside the track, I thought, No, not even he, the hated Albala, deserves such a sorrow."

The mounting deaths from typhus gave the death train its name. But the killer disease was only one of its scourges. Almost everyone suffered from dysentery, and many were unable to wait for one of the train's frequent stops to relieve themselves. Others were too weak to crawl down from the cars. So the latrine buckets overflowed, and the cars became open sewers.

The passengers were ill, too, with pleurisy and tuberculosis, diseases that spread easily when people coughed or spit. And many had wounds that, like Marion's, failed to heal.

"It was impossible," Marion said, "to keep the large burned area of my leg clean. It continued to ooze pus and was attacked by lice that I removed one by one and destroyed. Many people shaved their heads to be rid of the lice that we had carried with us from the camp, and that were surely on the train as well when we boarded it. But I begged Mama not to shave mine. So she carefully combed out the head lice several times a day, as she had done in Bergen-Belsen."

By April 15 the slow-moving train had traveled only as far as Lüneburg, about fifty miles northeast of Bergen. Often it stopped during the day in wooded areas to hide from the Allied aircraft that flew overhead.

Although the Germans attached a white flag to the train, the Allies had no idea of the innocent cargo it carried. Dive-bombings and strafings with machine guns continued, and sometimes the train was even caught in artillery crossfire. If the attacks came by day, the train stopped, and if the doors were opened, those who could run sought cover in nearby ditches. During night attacks the cars remained sealed, and the prisoners could only huddle in their places and hope for the best.

A few days later the train crossed the Elbe River, heading in an easterly and then a southeasterly direction. Soon after it had reached the far side of the river, the bridge on which it had traveled was blown up by Allied bombers. The train was now in the zone between the Western Allies and the Russians. It was, in fact, headed toward Berlin, the German capital, where Hitler still held out.

"By this time," Ruth reported, "so many had died of typhus that we were once again able to find a little room for ourselves in the cars. Our bread and water were long since gone. But the great number of stops made it possible for us to dig some potatoes, beets, and other root vegetables from the edges of fields. Water for drinking was our main problem. Some people drank from the creeks and streams along the tracks. But this was dangerous, for it could lead to severe diarrhea. So once, when the train stopped, I went up front to the locomotive and begged water from the German engineer. He did me a great kindness in letting me have as much water as I had vessels for. The water came from the steam locomotive itself and was hot and rusty. But at least it was safe for us to drink."

After one week on the train the prisoners came in sight of the bombed-out capital of Berlin. Because of the extensive damage to the railway lines, it took two days to cross the city. The train had to stop frequently to be backed up and rerouted wherever there were broken tracks, derailed cars, disabled locomotives, or heaps of rubble. The buildings that still stood appeared as weird silhouettes against the sky.

"These sights," Marion said, "all told us that the war must be coming to an end. Yet the Germans insisted on moving us onward along what was left of their railway system. It was senseless for them to do this, and it was terrifying to us. We could only conclude that they were determined to kill us, even in the midst of their own death throes."

After Berlin the train continued in a southerly direction, traveling almost parallel with the Polish border. The area had once been a rich farming belt. Although it now suffered from wartime shortages, the prisoners found it possible to obtain occasional handouts of bread and potatoes. An almost friendly SS man would accompany the groups of food seekers to a farmhouse door and wait there while they tried their luck.

Gradually the prisoners noticed that another favorable development was taking place. Some of the farmhouses had been recently abandoned. The German farm population was fleeing the area, a sure sign that the Russians, approaching from the East, must be close at hand.

"We were so ill and weak," Ruth said, "skeletons all of us, that we hardly realized what was happening. The train had become our 'home.' We crouched there like sick animals, sleeping, eating whatever we had, delousing ourselves and our clothing.

"Then one morning, very early, the doors were slid open. Men in uniforms sprang aboard, but they were not the SS. They spoke roughly in a strange accent, saying over and over again a word that sounded like the German for 'watch,' *'Uhr, Uhr!'*

"Some already had their arms full of wristwatches. Only a few of us had anything to give them, for we had long since bartered away everything we had for food. But they were good-natured about it. And when we looked out through the doors of the train, we saw that there were other Russian soldiers like them, marching alongside the track. They were leading away as prisoners our SS guards, or at least those SS who had not managed to escape during the night.

"We knew then that after six and a half years this was the day of our liberation from the Nazis. It was exactly two weeks since we had boarded the death train in Bergen-Belsen. The date was April twenty-third, 1945."

A Bergen-Belsen prisoner suffering from typhus, the disease that had killed tens of thousands at the camp by March 1945

April 1945, immediately after the liberation of Bergen-Belsen: women peeling potatoes while the unburied bodies of the dead lie in the background

The grave of Walter Blumenthal in Tröbitz, Germany, as it appeared at the time of his burial in June 1945

The marked burial site of Holocaust victim Walter Blumenthal, as a result of the work of caring and conscientious non-Jewish residents of Tröbitz

Entrance to the Honorary Jewish Cemetery that exists today in Tröbitz

Albert in Amsterdam, to which he commuted daily from Bussum while attending secondary school

Marion in Holland in December 1945, her shorn hair not yet fully grown back

At the Youth Aliyah home in Bussum, 1946: Albert in center and Marion, wearing glasses, at far right

In Peoria, Illinois, summer 1948: Albert with Marion, age thirteen and a half

Spring 1951: Marion, Ruth, and Albert in a park in Peoria

Marion's graduation from high school, June 1953

Marion and
Nathaniel's wedding,
August 2, 1953

Hoya, Germany, revisited by Albert Blumenthal in 1993

Albert on the bridge over the Weser, where Walter had proposed to Ruth in 1930

Albert and his wife, Diane, (near railing) in Hoya; behind them are the members of the Huth family who have written an outspoken account of Hoya's Jewish history, including the Holocaust and its aftermath

Marion with Ruth on December 20, 1994, Marion's 60th birthday; Ruth is in her eighty-seventh year

The Lazan family at a wedding on August 24, 2014. Left to right, top row: Rachel; Michael; Gavriel; Yoav; David; Ian. Middle row: Moshe, holding Rachel; Arielle, holding Leah Tova; Dahlia; Jordan Erica; Lisa; Hunter; Kasey Rose. Bottom row: Nathaniel; Marion; Allysa; Joshua; Susan; Rob.

Memorial blocks at Westerbork symbolizing the 102,000 prisoners who were deported from the transit camp during the Holocaust years. Those marked with Stars of David represent Jews; blocks representing gypsies and other groups are marked with different symbols

April 1995: Marion at Bergen-Belsen on the fiftieth anniversary of the liberation of the camp's suffering and dying victims

CHAPTER 7

"Freedom and Sorrow"

The liberation of the death train prisoners had taken place about a mile and a quarter from the small village of Tröbitz, in eastern Germany. At first many of the passengers hesitated to leave the train. They were too ill, too weak, or too timid to venture onto German soil on their own.

But the Russian soldiers soon made it clear that they had no supplies to share with the former prisoners and were, in fact, assigned to move on north toward Berlin. They also assured the refugees that most of the German population of Tröbitz had fled and that most of the abandoned farmhouses contained food, clothing, and bedding that were theirs for the taking.

"So before that day was out," Ruth said, "we left the train and headed for the village. Just as the Russians had said, many farmhouses were empty. In the first one I entered, I sniffed a faint but delicious smell of smoked meat. Following the scent, I climbed up to the sausages hanging around the rafters. At once I cut down a ham and brought it with me to the lower floor.

"Although we had not been deeply observant Jews when we lived in Germany, we had never eaten pork. But even Jewish law recognizes that there may be a time of great need. For us, this was the first plentiful protein we had had in years, and our bodies craved this nourishment. Marion was at this time ten and a half years old and weighted only thirty-five pounds. I myself weighed seventy-five pounds."

The Tröbitz farmhouses were well stocked, too, with milk, butter, cheese, and eggs. Pigs, cows, and even chickens had been left behind, as well as heavy jars of preserved fruits and vegetables.

Marion delighted in the sweet jams and preserves on the farmhouse shelves. But she soon learned that a shrunken stomach in a starved body must be fed very slowly and gradually. Many of the former prisoners fell too greedily on the rich and abundant food. Some actually died of the sudden overeating.

The farmhouse that the Blumenthals had entered became their new living quarters. "It was a small house," Marion remembered, "and we had it mostly to ourselves. Even though we could have spread out a little, we all slept in one room. Papa was in very poor health by this time, and my leg was still a raw and open wound. After huddling together on the train for two weeks, we feared the slightest separation. We wanted to stay as close to each other as my four perfect pebbles, the little stones that I could hold in the palm of my hand."

After the Russian liberators of the death train moved on, other Russian units arrived in Tröbitz to secure the conquered region for the formal occupation forces that were to follow. The military, too, foraged in the village and the surrounding countryside for food and other supplies, for they were often poorly equipped.

"In their crude way, though," Marion said, "the Russians tried to help us as best they could. They were extremely good to me, for each day they transported me to a nearby Russian Army field hospital, where they treated my leg. First they would clean the wound, and then they would sprinkle it with a greenish yellow powder. Mama and I believed that this powder was a form of penicillin, a miracle drug for infections that had been discovered before the war.

"As the first weeks in Tröbitz went by, we noticed that new skin was beginning to form around the large burned area of the wound. Mama and I were sure that the nourishing diet, including milk, eggs, and meat, that I was now eating was also helping my body to renew itself.

"But there was little that could be done to help my nightmares go away. Every day at the hospital I heard the cries of pain of both soldiers and civilians who had been maimed in the war. Worst of all, I saw the ugly stumps of the amputees. It was only then that I allowed myself to realize how close I had come to having my own leg amputated. These terrors haunted my nights in the farmhouse. I'm sure that was one reason why we all remained sleeping in the one room."

Despite their newfound freedom, the Tröbitz refugees continued to suffer a serious threat to their lives. Of the 2,500 prisoners who had boarded the death train at Bergen-Belsen, several hundred had died of typhus before reaching Tröbitz. Some, delirious with fever, unaware of their surroundings, had been carried from the train to the village in hand carts.

In the first weeks at Tröbitz new cases began to break out, and the refugees realized that the germ-bearing lice were still with them. Many who had not already shaved their heads did so, in order to deprive the lice of a place to hide and breed. And Marion, at last, allowed Mom to shave hers.

On May 7, 1945, the villagers learned from the radio of Germany's surrender. The war in Europe was at an end. Rejoicing was mixed with concern, however, for the Russian occupation forces now informed the refugees that they would have to remain in Tröbitz until the typhus epidemic had abated. A quarantine period of roughly two months was imposed. During that time none of the former prisoners would be allowed to leave Germany.

"We tried to settle down to some kind of life in that place," Marion said. "As the food that had remained in the farmhouses was consumed, people began to go on foot or by bicycle to quite distant farms and villages to beg, borrow, or trade in order to keep their families nourished. My brother, Albert, was an expert at this. He was always off somewhere scrounging for food and other necessities. In many ways, although only twelve and a half years old, he was becoming the provider of our family. For since the journey on the death train, Papa's health had worsened.

"Before our life in the camps Papa was a proud and disciplined man, always very exacting and in control of every situation. During Bergen-Belsen, especially, it must have hurt him terribly to watch his family suffer and to be unable to help us. Once he had been a heroic defender of his country and a respected businessman, as well as a loving and caring husband and father. But the Nazi system had broken him down and robbed him of his self-esteem. Yet he continued to have hope, always carrying with him the German-English dictionary from which he studied. For he still planned that one day we all would go to America."

As spring came to the Tröbitz countryside, freshly grown vegetables began to be available, and the food supply improved. The month of May also saw a decline in the number of typhus deaths. At last the disease seemed to have run its course, and the refugees began to look forward to returning to their home countries. For the Blumenthals repatriation would mean a return to Holland.

But suddenly, as May warmed into June, the number of typhus cases began to mount again. "And this time," Marion said, "Papa was one of its victims. Just as the Germans had tried to kill us in their own last moments, so this last gasp of the typhus epidemic would not let Papa go.

"For days he lay in the farmhouse bedroom, suffering from the burning fever, the stabbing headaches, the weird fantasies and semiconsciousness of the disease. And then, one morning, Albert went to his bedside and saw that he was dead.

"I think we all were numb with the shock of Papa's death. We had come so far, through flight, imprisonment, evacuation, the Nazis' final attempt to destroy us, liberation at last, and now this—freedom and sorrow.

"Mama, too, had been stricken with typhus and was in the early weak stage of recovery. My leg was still in need of treatment, and I could not walk without difficulty. So the task of burying Papa was left to Albert.

"By this time the telescope graves had been replaced by single graves, dug in a row just outside the wall of the Tröbitz village cemetery. There was no possibility of obtaining a coffin for Papa's body. Albert simply wrapped him in the bed sheet on which he'd lain when he died. This became his shroud.

"Then, with the help of two former prisoners who had been on the train with us, my brother placed Papa's body onto a wheeled cart, with two handles in front and two in back. The men helped him to trundle the cart to the cemetery.

"There Albert dug a shallow grave, perhaps four or five feet deep. He placed Papa's body in the earth, covered it, and laid bricks all around it, end to end, to mark the site. The date of Papa's death was June seventh, 1945."

One day after Walter Blumenthal was buried, the Tröbitz residents were notified abruptly that their quarantine period had come to an end. They were given two hours to gather their belongings and board the column of trucks that awaited them. They were about to begin the first stage of repatriation to their former homelands. Although the Blumenthals were not Dutch citizens, their refugee status would take them back to Holland, the country to which they had fled after leaving Germany.

Somehow Mama and Marion were helped onto the back of one of the open trucks. Albert was to join them. But as usual he was out somewhere gathering a supply of food for the journey. As the time for departure came closer, Mama wrung her hands in despair. What if something had now befallen Albert? Where *was* he?

At the very last moment he came running with his knapsack full, and he clambered aboard. Hands reached out to steady him. But suddenly the truck lurched forward. The jolt loosened Albert's grip on the heavy knapsack, and it flew off his shoulders and bounced onto the road. There it lay, in a receding cloud of dust, as the truck picked up speed.

"So," Marion said, "Albert lost his treasured knapsack, which he had had with him since Westerbork. But this was nothing compared with what we and so many others were leaving behind. There, in the Tröbitz cemetery, lay well over one hundred dead, plus hundreds more in the mass graves on the outskirts of the town and beside the railroad embankment. All told, at least six hundred people—one-quarter of the twenty-five hundred prisoners who had boarded the death train in Bergen-Belsen— had perished from disease or exhaustion."

CHAPTER 8

"Holland Again"

"Once more," Ruth said, "we arrived in Holland as refugees, homeless and penniless. The first time had been in January 1939, two months after *Kristallnacht* and Walter's imprisonment in Buchenwald.

"Now it was the summer of 1945. Six and a half years had passed. We had just barely managed to survive the camps. Walter was dead, and I was a widow at the age of thirty-seven. My worry about my two young children was the only thing that gave me the strength to face the future. And yes, there was a new name for us. We were no longer 'refugees.' Now we were 'displaced persons.' To put it more accurately, we were stateless."

Marion's memories of the return to Holland were more pleasant than Mama's and more filled with hope. "I remember," she said, "that after we left Tröbitz, we stopped at Leipzig, a much larger place, also in eastern Germany. There was an army hospital there where my leg, still very painful, was given further treatment. The weather was very hot. I recall sitting at a long wooden table and being served cold beer in large mugs. It was not unusual in Europe to give children and even babies a little beer to drink to nourish their bodies. My body must have craved this nourishment, for the beer tasted delicious.

"Later in the journey we stopped at a cloister near Maastricht, the Dutch city that is wedged between Belgium and Germany. I thought it was very exciting to be able to stand with one leg in Holland and one in Belgium, while waving an arm in farewell in the direction of Germany.

"From there we went on to Amsterdam. Although the city had suffered much during the war and many of its trees had been cut down for firewood, it seemed a very luxurious place to me. On our arrival we stayed briefly with Papa's cousins, whom I knew as Tante Gerda and Uncle Ernst. Uncle Ernst de

Levie was Jewish, but Tante Gerda, who was not, had managed to conceal his identity from the Nazis during the war. I thought that they and their seventeen-year-old daughter, Ingrid, were the most handsome people I had ever known.

"Tante Gerda wore her smooth dark hair in a French knot, known as a chignon, at the nape of her neck. She understood at once how much I craved small treats of food and clothing. I was still scrawny and underweight, and my hair had not yet grown in. Also I wore glasses, which I'd had to wear from the age of four because my eye muscles were not in balance. As a result of this problem, I was slightly cross-eyed."

Marion could vividly recall the de Levies's second-floor apartment in a tall, narrow Amsterdam building. Although their home was comfortably furnished, the de Levies, like other Dutch citizens, still suffered from war shortages. All clothing was rationed, and coupons had to be saved up. But Tante Gerda managed to buy Marion her first piece of new clothing, a flower-patterned summer dress. Another hard-to-obtain item was chewing gum. Marion was intrigued with this unusual confection, and when Uncle Ernst offered her an allowance equivalent to about ten cents a week, she eagerly saved her coins to buy a single Chiclet.

"I don't know how many weeks," Marion said, "I kept that one piece of chewing gum. Each day I would chew it, carefully wrap it up, and then chew it again the next day. I also remember how upset I became when I got a stain on the flowered dress that Tante Gerda had bought me. I wore it one day on an outing to an amusement park where I rode the carousel. As the painted horse on which I was seated went up and down, I must have hit my chin. As a result my tooth bit into my lip, causing some drops of blood to fall on my beautiful new dress. Tante Gerda, though, was not angry. She was comforting and reassuring, all of which made me feel even more unhappy and undeserving."

The stay with the de Levie family could not last, however. Soon Mama and Marion and Albert were transferred to a former Jewish convalescent home in Amsterdam. The eight-story building had been converted into a temporary shelter for seventy-five to one hundred displaced persons.

Although the accommodations were simple, life was no longer filled with fear and uncertainty. Hunger had ceased to be an everyday sensation. And it was possible to bathe, to wear freshly washed clothing, even to brush one's teeth every morning. In October Albert reached his thirteenth birthday and became Bar Mitzvah in a small, quiet ceremony at an Amsterdam synagogue. So that he would have a special gift to mark the occasion, Mama sold Papa's pocket watch and bought Albert a ring.

Mama's worries about the family's future were far from over, however. The children needed to be educated, and Ruth herself had no way of providing a livelihood for the three of them. Perhaps, she reasoned, Papa's plan of emigrating to Palestine was the best idea after all.

Hundreds of thousands of displaced Jews—broken and impoverished families like the Blumenthals—hoped to be able to make a new start in Palestine. True, the British were still limiting immigration to only about fifteen hundred a month, and conditions in the desertlike land were harsh and often inhospitable. But there *were* plans afoot to develop a Jewish state in Palestine, one that would become a permanent home for the Jews.

"So, soon after Albert's Bar Mitzvah," Marion said, "he and I were sent to a Youth Aliyah home in the small town of Bussum, about an hour's train ride south of Amsterdam. There we were to be prepared for aliyah, or immigration, to the future Jewish homeland. We would be taught both the Hebrew language and the Orthodox religion.

"The home was on spacious grounds with a vegetable

garden, chickens, and rabbits. And Albert and I had the company of the twenty or so other children, ranging in age from eight to eighteen. Some were orphans, while others, like us, had one surviving parent.

"Mr. and Mrs. Birnbaum, who ran the home and did the teaching, were also survivors of Westerbork and Bergen-Belsen. They had six children, two of whom were close in age to Albert and me: their daughter, Susi, and their son, Zvi."

While living and studying at the Youth Aliyah home, Marion also began her secular education in Dutch at a nearby Montessori school. The teaching was patient and caring. Dutch was a new language for eleven-year-old Marion, as was Hebrew. Before that she had known only German. Albert, too, was now learning Dutch. He and Zvi Birnbaum, along with other teenagers from the home, commuted daily by train to a secondary school in Amsterdam.

Ruth, meantime, remained in Amsterdam. She had moved in with Walter's sister Rosi, who had lived in hiding in Holland during the war, and she was studying to become a beautician and manicurist. It was during this time that Uncle Ernst offered to have Marion's eye condition corrected.

"I'm so ashamed now," Marion said, "when I think of how

I behaved. Uncle Ernst arranged for me to come to Amsterdam by train. As this was to be a surprise for my mother, he met me at the station and took me to the hospital where the operation was to be performed. I was, of course, quite nervous. But I was also happy at the thought of having my eyes 'straightened' and perhaps not having to wear glasses anymore.

"At the hospital Uncle Ernst put me in the hands of the nurses who were to prepare me for the operation. Somehow I was left lying on the stretcher in a room all by myself for what seemed like a very long time. No one came to my side; no one was there to reassure me. Suddenly I was seized with panic. Maybe it was my years in the camps that told me that I must escape and save myself. In any case, I jumped up from the stretcher, found my belongings, ran all the way to the railway station, and returned to Bussum.

"What a terrible thing to do! But patient and kind as always, Uncle Ernst understood the reason for my flight. The surgery was rescheduled, and this time he insisted on being allowed to remain at my side until I was wheeled into the operating room. Mama, too, was there, and the operation was a success. I recovered quickly, and my eyes were soon able to function normally."

● ● ●

Ruth finally completed her beautician's training and received her certification, qualifying her to give facials, manicures, and pedicures. Learning the terminology for the muscles and tissues in Dutch had been difficult for her, but she was determined to succeed. Once she was certified, she bought a bicycle to travel to the homes of her clients.

Her visits with Marion and Albert, however, were limited to once a week at most. Either she came to Bussum by train or the children traveled to Amsterdam.

"Even though the Birnbaums were like second parents to us, and Susi became my dear friend, which she has remained to this day," Marion said, "I was terribly lonely for my mother. I had learned in Bergen-Belsen to suppress my feelings and not to cry out even in physical pain. So I kept these deep anxieties to myself in order not to worry my mother. But often I was close to hysteria, and I could hear my heart pounding in my chest as if it were about to burst."

As the time drew closer for the planned voyage from Holland to Palestine, the Blumenthals learned that the immigration was to be a children's transport only and that the group would have to travel illegally by way of the island of Cyprus, in the eastern Mediterranean. Ruth would not be allowed to accompany Marion and Albert. She would have to make her own arrangements and hope to arrive at a later date.

"After all we had been through," Mama said, "I could not possibly risk such a separation. Often the illegal ships were old and leaky, and if the British came upon such a ship, they would force it to return to Europe. How could I put my children's lives in danger again? So at once I went about seeing what we could do to emigrate as a family to the United States, as Walter and I had originally intended."

Again it was necessary to obtain an affidavit from a family member or other sponsor in America, as well as a visa and other papers. This time the affidavit was generously offered by a brother of Tante Rosi's husband, a warm and caring man whom the Blumenthals had never met. His name was Arnold Wolf. The remaining arrangements took time. But there was one piece of very good news. The Holland-America Line still had it on record that the Blumenthals had paid their passage for four in 1938, when they first planned to sail from Rotterdam to New York on the *Nieuw Amsterdam*.

Now, nearly ten years later, the passage money was still on deposit and could be applied to a sailing on the SS *Veendam*. The cost of the sailing had gone up, but Papa's share would be passed on to the others, and only a small sum needed to be added.

"What an exciting time," Marion said, "when we finally had everything in readiness and our passage date approached. It was April 1948. I was nearly thirteen and a half, had filled out and grown taller. Also, I had very definite ideas about what kind of wardrobe I wanted for the sailing and for my arrival in New York. Clothing and shoes were still rationed in Holland, so Mama and I had constant arguments about what items the valuable coupons should be used for.

"One thing I needed badly was a pair of new shoes. Mama had to give up her shoe coupon so that I could have them, and of course she felt I should choose a pair of sensible black or brown leather oxfords. By this time we were buying my shoes one size too big because I was growing so rapidly. When I looked at those terrible 'canalboats' Mama wanted me to get, I was practically in tears.

"As usual we argued back and forth. But my will had become stronger than ever, and finally I won. When I boarded the *Veendam* a week or so later, I was wearing a pair of fashionable navy blue slip-on pumps. I felt completely ready for New York and my new life in America."

For Marion and Albert the ten-day voyage was luxurious

beyond anything they had ever known. The shipboard food was abundant, varied, delicious, and beautifully served. Marion could not get over the many flavors and colors of ice cream, a dessert that was available at almost any time of day. If this was a foretaste of life in America, she was sure that it was going to suit her perfectly.

On the evening before the *Veendam* was to land, the passengers were told to be on deck early next morning if they wished to see the approach into New York Harbor.

"Mama, Albert, and I," Marion said, "were part of the huge crowd that started to gather as early as five A.M., all of us craning our necks for a first view of the Statue of Liberty. When the tall figure of that longed-for symbol of freedom appeared, I became too choked to speak. So many emotions seized me at once: joy and gratitude, bitterness for the cruelties we and so many others had suffered, and deep sadness that Papa could not share this moment with us. He would never know that we had reached America at last.

"The date of our landing was April twenty-third, 1948. By coincidence, it was exactly three years to the day since we had been liberated from the death train by the Russians."

CHAPTER 9

"America, at Last"

The *Veendam* docked at Hoboken, New Jersey. There Mama, Marion, and Albert were met by the family of Papa's sister Clara, who, with her husband and daughter, had emigrated to the United States in 1938. The Blumenthals were taken directly to Tante Clara's small, immaculate apartment on West 161st Street in the Washington Heights section of Manhattan.

"From the moment we left the ship," Marion recalled, "I was in a state of bewilderment and awe. No city in Germany or Holland had ever had so many tall buildings as New York, so much motor traffic, so many people, such noisy, bustling streets.

And I had yet to ride in the fast-moving elevator of a skyscraper or to descend into the rattling and screeching subways.

"Immediately I found a friend in my cousin Helga, who was a few years younger than I. She shared her pastimes and her companions with me. Tante Clara meantime tried to make us as comfortable as possible. She cooked us delicious meals. I had only one fault to find. We had arrived in America just as the Passover holiday, with its many food restrictions, was about to begin.

"I could make do with eating matzoh, our unleavened bread, instead of raised bread. But many sweets that I'd been looking forward to were not kosher for Passover. Above all, here in the land of chewing gum—slim sugary sticks in many flavors and Chiclets galore—I had to wait eight whole days for the holiday to be over before I could indulge my craving.

"Bubble gum was a new variation that fascinated me. A few weeks later, when I learned to use the subways, I sat gazing in wonder at the huge bubbles that some of my fellow passengers were able to blow. Almost as dramatic were the sharp, cracking sounds they made as their jaws clamped down on the gum.

"I soon learned that to chew gum, especially in public, is not a very mannerly thing to do. I suppose it was the abundance of it in the United States as compared to its scarcity in postwar Holland that impressed me so."

Like the Blumenthals' brief stay with the de Levie family in Amsterdam, their time at Tante Clara's in New York soon came to an end. As kind as their relatives had been in both instances, Ruth knew that she and her children must somehow make their own way.

On arriving in the United States, the Blumenthals had registered with HIAS, the Hebrew Immigrant Aid Society. While HIAS tried to find a Jewish community that could offer the newcomers a place to live and a temporary means of support, the organization moved them into a residence hotel on Manhattan's 116th Street.

"The three of us," Marion said, "lived in one room, with a bathroom in the corridor that we shared with the other families. As there were no proper cooking facilities, our meals became very peculiar. Albert had developed a terrific appetite for canned fruit cocktail. It was nothing for him to finish a sixteen-ounce can at one sitting and go right on to open another.

"I, on the other hand, had a passion for fatty foods. My

favorite was a big jar of mayonnaise into which I dipped one potato chip after another, out of the biggest bag I could find. It was no wonder I was putting on weight. At the age of ten and a half, just after our liberation, I had weighted thirty-five pounds. Now, in the spring of 1948, at age thirteen and a half I weighed one *hundred* and thirty-five. In three years I had gained a hundred pounds!"

Ruth was quietly indulgent of the eating habits of her two teenagers. She did not take as much pleasure as they did, however, in the American snack foods or in other aspects of American popular culture. She was far too taken up with worry about the problem of starting over. She had no money and no job skills that she could apply without a knowledge of English. She felt completely lost in her new surroundings. "To me," Ruth confessed, "the future looked bleak."

The Blumenthals had been rooming in the Manhattan residence hotel only a few weeks when they were notified that HIAS had found them a more permanent place to live. It was being offered by the Jewish Community Council in Peoria, Illinois.

"Peoria," Marion said. "We had never heard of Peoria. I'm not even sure we knew enough about American geography at the time to have heard of Illinois. New York itself was strange and new to us. But at least we had relatives there. In Peoria we wouldn't know anybody.

"However, we had no choice, if we did not accept the free housing and the chance for work and schooling in Peoria, we would lose our HIAS sponsorship and would be entirely on our own. Without a proper wage earner in the family, there was no way for us to survive financially. So we packed our few belongings and set off by train for the American Midwest."

On arriving in Peoria in June 1948, Ruth, Marion, and Albert discovered that their apartment, in a rundown part of town, was to be shared with two other families. Everyone would have to take turns using the single bathroom and preparing meals in the kitchen, which was equipped with an old-fashioned wooden icebox. But at least here was an opportunity for the newcomers to establish themselves in an American community.

"That very summer," Marion said, "each of us got a job. Mama, finding nothing else open to her, started work as a housekeeper for a prosperous family in town, the Hokins. Albert was hired by a local jewelry store. He scrubbed the floors and cleaned and polished the showcases and counters. And I went to work in a laundry, sorting and folding clothes, for twenty cents an hour. I also began to take lessons in English.

"In September I entered public school in Peoria. I was still so far behind in English, however, that I was placed in fourth grade. There I was, a thirteen-year-old among nine-year-olds. Not only was I four years older than my classmates, but I had also grown plump and was beginning to mature.

"My teacher tried to be helpful. But she was a rather nervous person, as I recall, and she spoke very rapidly. I could not help feeling out of place and uncomfortable. Although I excelled in mathematics and in European geography, English was my big stumbling block. Along with Dutch and Hebrew, it was my third new language in three years."

Albert was also wrestling with English at school. Yet both young people continued at their jobs, putting in as many after-school hours as they could, for every penny counted. Ruth's work at the Hokins' brought in some extras, too, for her employer was generous with take-home food and with hand-me-down clothing for Marion that was still in fine condition.

"In December 1948," Marion recalled, "we celebrated our first Hanukkah in Peoria. This eight-day Festival of Lights fell close to my fourteenth birthday. So Albert bought me a special gift, one that was typical of the new luxuries that were available to us in America.

"When I opened the box, however, I was so disappointed that I actually started to cry. I suppose I had expected a box of elegant chocolates or some other confectionary treat. Instead he had bought me a pair of sheer, flesh-colored nylon stockings.

"Nylons had first made their appearance in America shortly before the war. Then, as the 'miracle' fiber was needed for parachutes and other war materials, it had become unavailable. Now, in 1948, everybody was clamoring for nylon hosiery. But to me, getting my first pair of nylons was a sign of having to grow up, of becoming a young woman.

"This I was not ready to do. I was not ready to say farewell to the childhood I had never had. I wanted sweets and games. I wanted to be as carefree as my nine-year-old classmates, who knew nothing of the deadly concentration camp in which I had spent the ninth and tenth years of *my* childhood."

The following year saw an all-around improvement in the lives of the Blumenthals. Ruth learned that her longtime skills as a seamstress had good earning power, and she went to work for a local tailor. Later she advanced to an even better job doing alterations and custom tailoring for a downtown Peoria department store.

Albert, who had enrolled in Peoria Central High School, had kept his job in the jewelry store and even gotten a raise. He worked his way up to an assistant clerkship, increasing his earnings from thirty-five to fifty-five cents an hour.

Marion not only held on to her job in the laundry but began to earn additional money as a baby-sitter. By pooling their earnings and living very frugally, the Blumenthals were now able to move from the community-sponsored quarters in Peoria to a modest apartment of their own. But best of all for Marion was her progress at school.

"By getting extra help with English after school and by attending summer school, I was skipped that fall to junior high. For the first time I had that wonderful feeling of belonging. Happily I had also gotten some good advice from one of the mothers for whom I baby-sat. She noticed my tendency to eat too-rich foods, as a way of compensating for my years of hunger, and she gently advised me about the importance of maintaining a good appearance.

"I listened to her, as I might not have to my own mother,

and I soon began to slim down. Being accepted by the boys and girls in my class was enough compensation for me."

The Blumenthals found that Peoria was turning out to be a comfortable and secure place to live after all. There were varied opportunities for employment, there was a good public school system, and there was a Jewish religious community. By the time Marion was in high school, she was working part-time in one of the city's department stores.

"I sold housedresses at Szold's Department Store," she recalled, "one for a dollar fifty-nine, two for three dollars. The store was owned by Henrietta Szold's nephews. Henrietta Szold, who had died in 1945 at the age of eighty-five, was one of the founders of Hadassah, which was organized in 1912 to promote a Jewish homeland in Palestine. She was the first president of Hadassah and also the director of a Youth Aliyah program, similar to the one we'd taken part in in Holland.

"Albert and I had also started to teach Sunday school classes, which brought in a few extra dollars. Somehow we seemed to find time for work, school, *and* a bit of social life. I also became more active in the Peoria religious community and began to attend synagogue services."

• • •

The High Holy Days of 1951 found Marion seated in the women's balcony of Peoria's Orthodox synagogue. In this branch of the Jewish faith it was traditional for men and women to be separated at services. But a small section at the rear of the balcony had been reserved for students attending Peoria's Bradley University.

"I will always remember what I was wearing on the fast day of Yom Kippur that autumn. It was a knitted navy blue wool jersey dress, with an embroidered motif in red near the right shoulder. The dress was a hand-me-down that I had been lucky to receive, for I could never have afforded something as lovely as that new.

"A number of Bradley students, mostly young men, were gathered behind us. When I glanced around, I noticed one who was staring at me intently. I tried to put my mind on the services, but it was hard not to take just one more look. When I did, his eyes were still on me.

"I was sixteen at the time and a sophomore in high school. I had only recently started dating and was enjoying going out with a variety of boys. I never dreamed of getting serious with any one person. I was certain that that would not happen for years to come."

When the service ended, the young man approached Marion and asked her, very politely, if he could walk her home from the synagogue. As they strolled along on that Yom Kippur afternoon, Marion learned that the young man's home was in the Long Island, New York, community of Woodmere, a place that she had never heard of.

He had fine manners and spoke lovingly of his family back home, consisting of his parents and his sister, Naomi. He himself was nineteen and had three more years of college.

"Somehow," Marion said, "I knew even then that this person was someone special. Already my new admirer seemed to have made up his mind that we were meant for each other. And, as our courtship continued, lengthening into a period of almost two years, I began to realize that he was the man with whom I would spend the rest of my life. His name was Nathaniel Lazan."

EPILOGUE

In June 1953 Marion Blumenthal graduated from Peoria Central High School. She was eighteen and a half and was rated eighth in scholarly achievement in a graduating class of 265 students.

Nathaniel's parents visited from New York and joined Mama and Albert in attending the graduation. Nathaniel had just finished his junior year at Bradley and had to complete one more year of college for his degree. Yet he had convinced both his parents and Marion's family that the young couple should marry that summer.

On August 2, 1953, Marion Blumenthal and Nathaniel Lazan were married in New York. Their first child, David Walter, was born in 1955, their daughter, Susan, in 1957, and their third child, Michael, in 1960. Today Marion and her husband have eight grandchildren. They have made their home for many years in Hewlett, New York.

For the past fifteen years Marion has been giving talks and interviews about her Holocaust experience to both children and adults in schools and other settings, and has at last been able to put her story into book form. On completion of this undertaking, one more challenge awaited her: that of revisiting the sites and scenes of her childhood. In April 1995, on the occasion of the fiftieth anniversary of her family's liberation from the Nazis, Marion Blumenthal Lazan, accompanied by her husband, her daughter Susan, and her son Michael, reunited with other Westerbork and Bergen-Belsen survivors in Holland and Germany. In addition to the former concentration camps, the Lazans visited the grave of Marion's father in Tröbitz and Marion's hometown of Hoya.

Although she approached her journey with deep anxiety, Marion soon found herself responding positively to her German hosts. Especially moving was the reception tendered to the Lazans in Hoya by the Huth family: Heike and Hans and their teenage daughter and son, Sara and Henning. As conscientious German residents, the Huths had taken on a postwar research project to reconstruct the history of the town's Jewish community. In 1992 the fruits of their study, tracing Jewish life in Hoya from 1754 to the Holocaust and its aftermath, were published in a volume titled *Wann wird man je versteh'n* . . . [*When will People Ever Understand?*]. Similarly, in Tröbitz, a local historian, Erika Arlt, has made it her mission to research and compile a history of the death train. Also, the graves of those Jews who were laid to rest in Tröbitz have been looked after since the late 1940s by the cemetery's German caretaker, Heinz Färber. Today this German village has the rare distinction of having the Honorary Jewish Cemetery in which there are seventy-nine individually marked burial sites. Here, unlike the mass burial sites of almost all Holocaust victims, the names of the dead are recorded for posterity.

Albert Blumenthal and his wife, Diane, reside in Atherton, California, where he is a financial consultant. His advanced degrees include an M.B.A. in finance and marketing from Northwestern University. In 1958, while on army duty in Europe, he made his first visit to Hoya, the town in Germany where he had been born. The fate of its Jewish community was then unknown, and its Jewish cemetery was in ruins. Subsequent visits took place in 1983 and again in 1993, at which time he also visited the sites of Westerbork and Bergen-Belsen and his father's grave at Tröbitz.

Ruth Blumenthal Meyberg remained in Peoria until 1956 and subsequently lived in California and in New York, where she still resides. In her eighty-seventh year she is a spirited, energetic woman. A survivor in the truest sense, she continues to be a vital presence in the lives of those she sustained through the Holocaust and its aftermath.

BIBLIOGRAPHY

Boas, Jacob. *Boulevard des Misères: The Story of Transit Camp Westerbork*. Hamden, CT:
Archon Books, 1985.

Epstein, Helen. *Children of the Holocaust: Conversations with Sons and Daughters of
Survivors*. New York: G. P. Putnam's Sons, 1979.

Frank, Anne. *The Diary of Anne Frank: The Critical Edition. Prepared by the Netherlands
State Institute for War Documentation*. New York: Doubleday, 1989.

Gilbert, Martin. *The Holocaust: A History of the Jews of Europe During the Second World War*.
New York: Holt, Rinehart, and Winston, 1985.

Hillesum, Etty. *Letters from Westerbork*. New York: Pantheon Books, 1986.

Höss, Rudolf. *The Memoirs of the SS Kommandant at Auschwitz*. New York:
Prometheus Books, 1992.

Laqueur, Walter. *The Terrible Secret: Suppression of the Truth About Hitler's "Final Solution."*
Boston: Little, Brown, 1993.

Lipstadt, Deborah E. *Denying the Holocaust: The Growing Assault on Truth and Memory*.
New York: The Free Press, 1993.

Lookstein, Haskel. *Were We Our Brothers' Keepers? The Public Response of American Jews
to the Holocaust 1938–1944*. New York: Vintage Books, 1988.

Mechanicus, Philip. *Year of Fear: A Jewish Prisoner Waits for Auschwitz*. New York:
Hawthorn Books, 1968.

Meltzer, Milton. *Never to Forget: The Jews of the Holocaust*. New York:
Harper & Row, 1976.

Presser, Jacob. *Ashes in the Wind: The Destruction of Dutch Jewry*. Detroit: Wayne State University Press, 1988.

Regional Centre for Political Education in Lower Saxony. *Bergen-Belsen: Text and Pictures of the Memorial Exhibition*. Hanover, Germany, 1991.

Schloss, Eva, with Evelyn Julia Kent. *Eva's Story: A Survivor's Tale by the Stepsister of Anne Frank*. New York: St. Martin's Press, 1989.

Verdoner-Sluizer, Hilde. *Signs of Life: The Letters of Hilde Verdoner-Sluizer from Nazi Transit Camp Westerbork, 1942–1944*. Washington, D.C.: Acropolis Books, 1990.

Weinberg, Werner. *Self-Portrait of a Holocaust Survivor*. Jefferson, NC: McFarland, 1985.

Wyden, Peter. *Stella: One Woman's True Tale of Evil, Betrayal, and Survival in Hitler's Germany*. New York: Simon and Schuster, 1992.

Wyman, David S. *Abandonment of the Jews: America and the Holocaust, 1941–1945*. New York: Pantheon Books, 1984.

GERMANY AND SURROUNDING NATIONS, 2016

North Sea

Baltic Sea

Amsterdam

Westerbork

Bussum
NETHERLANDS

Rotterdam

Hamburg

Bremen

Hoya • Bergen-Belsen

Celle

Berlin

Hanover

Brakel

Tröbitz

POLAND

to
Auschwitz

Maastricht

BELGIUM

GERMANY

Buchenwald

Terezín

Prague

CZECH
REPUBLIC

Frankfurt

Nuremberg

Strasbourg

Stuttgart

Munich

AUSTRIA

Salzburg

FRANCE

SWITZERLAND

Afterword to Twentieth Anniversary Edition

It's hard to believe that twenty years have passed since the publication of *Four Perfect Pebbles* in 1996. So much has happened in my life these past two decades, as is true for many of us.

There would be no afterword had I not had the help of my dear friend and coauthor, Lila Perl, who sadly passed away in December of 2013. It is because of Lila's efforts, talent, and diligence that *Four Perfect Pebbles* has reached more than a million readers since publication.

Four Perfect Pebbles has taken on a life of its own—and definitely changed my life for the better! The book has been translated into German, Hebrew, Dutch, and Japanese, which is tremendously exciting, of course. The Dutch version is of special relevance: Gerton van Boom, a Dutch businessman, publisher, and philanthropist, took it upon himself to print 102,000 copies with the title *Vier gelijke stenen Op de vlucht voor de holocaust.*

Why 102,000 copies? To symbolize and remember the 102,000 men, women, and children, out of a total population of 120,000 Dutch Jews, who were deported from Camp Westerbork and destined never to return. My family and I were among the small percentage of "lucky ones" who did return. Gerton van Boom placed this large number of books at the disposal of the Camp Westerbork Museum in the Netherlands, to be given free of charge to visitors. A second printing was soon needed!

I have come to understand that my story is one of survival and continuity. In the epilogue of the original edition, my beloved mother, of blessed memory, is described as an active and energetic eighty-seven-year-old. She was *almost* as active and energetic to the very end, and still living in her own apartment, when she passed from this life six weeks short of her 105th birthday. No words can describe my incredible mother, a "lady to the *n*th degree."

Yes, *survival and continuity.* Leah Tova, my mother's

great-great-granddaughter (and our great-granddaughter), who when born gave our family five generations of tough but gentle women.

As of this writing, in addition to our three married children, David (married to Lisa), Susan (married to Rob), Michael (married to Rachel), we have nine grandchildren, three of whom are married: Arielle (married to Moshe), Joshua (married to Allysa), Gavriel (married to Ariela), Dahlia, Yoav, Jordan Erica, Hunter, Ian, and Kasey Rose, and two great-(really great!) granddaughters, Leah Tova and Rachel Tehilla.

Some ten years ago, Dr. John Chua, an associate professor at Richmond University in London, wrote and directed the documentary *Marion's Triumph: Surviving History's Nightmare*, which aired on PBS. The film is about my Holocaust experiences and the work I do in schools and communities to share my story—and the universal message of love, tolerance, and respect for one another that I believe in so passionately.

When I look back at the many schools of every type (public, private, parochial, alternative, etc.) I have visited in thirty-eight states and abroad, I sometimes wonder how I've had the energy! I have personally reached more than a million youngsters and adults, and it has become my mission to reach even more. Many

people I speak to or meet have their own problems to deal with—
not being accepted, being a new immigrant, having a difficult
childhood, being homesick, and so many other issues—yet
somehow, because of my own background and perspective, I am
able to communicate to them a message of hope. Without hope,
it is almost impossible to live a healthy, happy, and productive
life. I finish each and every presentation by giving too many
hugs to count. Hugs have become my trademark!

I would be remiss not to mention John Holt of Pittsburgh,
who wrote a musical score about my life experiences, with a
title song called, "*Four Perfect Pebbles.*" This song is sung after each
of my presentations. John truly captured my feelings as a fearful
child, and I thank him.

Keys to the city have been presented to me! One mayor said,
"Although this key will not open up any doors in our city, you
have opened up the hearts of our citizens!" This past year, I was
honored to help plant two new trees, one in New York, the other
in New Jersey. Both ceremonies were particularly memorable.

On June 12, 2014, in Aurora, New York, I was privileged to
be the keynote speaker at an event commemorating what would
have been Anne Frank's eighty-fifth birthday. On that day, at
Emily Howland Elementary School, we planted a sapling from

the original chestnut tree that Anne looked down on so many years ago. I concluded my talk with the following prayer, hope, and wish:

May the roots of our Anne Frank Chestnut Sapling grow deep and strong

May its leaves give shade in a troubled world.

May the sight of this lovely tree

Give us the understanding and desire

To be kind, respectful, and tolerant towards one another.

In the spring of 2015, at the John Hill School in Boonton, New Jersey, I was given the wonderful surprise of having a tree planted in my honor. It was a dogwood tree, the official state memorial tree of New Jersey. Elaine Doherty, the school's PTA president, wrote a beautiful message about the dogwood tree. I would like to share her words with you:

"A tree is a symbol of an immense and enduring strength. The kind of strength we read about in *Four Perfect Pebbles*, and a strength we see in Marion Blumenthal Lazan as she spoke today.

"A tree is a protector and signifies life. A life lost or a life spared, both of which we honor today. Those who survived that horrible time in history and those who fell victim to it.

"A tree can represent the completion of a difficult period

and a return to stability. It signifies wishes fulfilled and all things representative of a family. We plant our tree for Marion's family, and all the families who were touched by the Holocaust.

"We have chosen to plant a dogwood tree. The dogwood tree is New Jersey's designated tree for remembrance celebrations. However, in our case, the dogwood tree was chosen for a much more symbolic reason.

"Each spring when the dogwood blooms, it will have hundreds of flowers made up of four petals, each round in shape and almost the same size. Some may say they are 'Four Perfect Petals.'

"So please, when the sun grows warm and we begin to emerge from school back to the fields to practice and play again, look to the courtyard and the Dogwood tree. Look for those 'Four Perfect Petals' that fill the branches, and remember back to what we read in Marion Blumenthal Lazan's memoir, *Four Perfect Pebbles.*"

Since the publication of *Four Perfect Pebbles*, I have been back to Germany on six occasions to speak in schools and churches. It has been a remarkable revelation to see how one German town, among others, is doing its best to redress the evil, crimes, and horrors perpetrated during the Nazi era. The study of the Holocaust in German schools is mandatory, and students are highly encouraged to visit the former camps.

The new Marion Blumenthal *Hauptschule* (high school) in my former hometown of Hoya, Germany, was named in my honor in 2010, and in 2014, I received honorary citizenship from Hoya, the town we had been forced to flee some seventy years earlier. Over the past ten years, *Stolpersteine* have been placed in Hoya and elsewhere in Germany. A *Stolperstein* is a brass plaque set in the sidewalk in front of a home where a deported Jew once lived. It gives the victim's name, date of birth, where, when, and how he or she died. There are four *Stolpersteine* in front of the house where we lived in Hoya, one for each of my grandparents, one for my father, and now one for my mother. *Stolpersteine* are a vivid and constant reminder of what happened on those streets, and they are hard to miss. Students from "my" school keep the *Stolpersteine* in Hoya clean and shiny.

As gratifying as the honors and recognition are, what is truly most rewarding and important to me is the audience's reaction after a presentation, and the letters and emails I receive from readers and from people I have met on my travels. Students who attended my talk years ago and are now teachers themselves have begun inviting me to speak to their students. *Survival and continuity.* They understand that this generation will be the last to hear personal, firsthand accounts of the Holocaust.

I would like to share with you several of the many letters I have received these past twenty years.

From a letter written by a former Catholic parochial student in San Francisco who saw me speak more than fifteen years ago, and is now an executive with Google:

"I remember your smile and the joy you brought to the room. I remember how your husband looked at you when you spoke. I remember going home and trying potato chips and mayo and I think I remember dogs? But most of all I remember your certainty. You were so sure of yourself and your mission in life. You survived hell and turned something weakening and negative into something strong and positive. You inspired me and continue to do so daily."

From a letter from a young immigrant and high school student:

"I'm from Mexico. I live with my parents and sister. When we came here, I didn't know any words in English, and had to take ESL in school because I didn't know how to speak English. But when you came to my school, to tell your story, I was listening, and at the same time, thinking that nothing is impossible. . . .You are an example for everybody; I'll never forget you."

From a letter from a high school foreign exchange student:

"At that time, I was really having problems fitting in and being happy with my host family, and my new school. I felt sad most of the time. I was always afraid of doing something wrong, and I was missing my family just so much.

"The day you visited us, I felt so moved by your story. You taught me and showed us all how courage to thrive can be found in awful situations and by that, taught me to cope when times are hard . . . my history teacher made arrangements for me to meet you afterward. I remember seeing you, and the smile you gave me, and right now, as I am writing this, I have goose-bumps and tears in my eyes, just to relive those memories. . . . For the first time, I started crying and told the truth, saying it was hard and that I missed my parents so much. You gave me a hug, and believe it or not, it was the first hug I received in the USA, and I just felt so good. You gave me hope. You said it would be great at the end. And I believed you. . . .

"So now, three years later, I am back in Brazil, with my parents, and I just got accepted to medical college, and I hope in the future to help people the most that I can. I am sending this message to thank you. Thank you, Marion, from the bottom of my heart. That day you meant the world for me and I am never going to forget you, or your story. Your kindness gave me the strength to carry on. God bless you and your family.

"With love, and the most sincere thank you, Filipe.

"P.S. Since that day, I have read *Four Perfect Pebbles* five times, and it is still my favorite book."

There you have it, my afterword.

I hope to continue my mission to reach out to young adults and communities for many years to come. I hope to continue to inspire people, to talk about understanding, tolerance, and empathy, with my loving husband of sixty-three years, Nathaniel, at my side. I hope to see my family grow in numbers and good deeds. I hope and pray that children, grandchildren, and all succeeding generations, everywhere, will be kind to one another, and grow up healthy, happy and productive, in a world of love and peace.

Hugs,

Marion

Marion's mother's passport, with a
large *J* stamped on it for "Jew"

Marion's father's passport, with a
large *J* stamped on it for "Jew".

The author, deep in the
midst of the concrete
blocks during a visit to
the Holocaust Museum
in Berlin

A "permission"
slip allowing the
Blumenthal family
to take a few items
out of the country

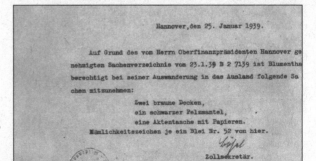

Gouda, Holland, early 1939. Marion's parents were assigned to look after a number of other young children sent by their parents to Holland to escape the Nazis. Marion is the little girl in the very front of the group

Marion's father's *Stolperstein embedded in* the sidewalk in front of the home where the Blumenthals lived in Hoya.

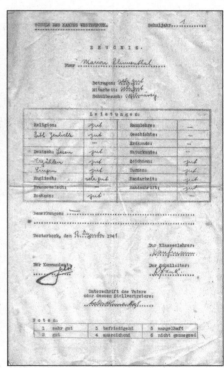

Marion's report card from Camp Westerbork in Holland, dated just after her seventh birthday

PRAISE FOR *FOUR PERFECT PEBBLES*

An ALA Notable Book

An ALA Quick Pick for Reluctant Readers

An IRA Young Adults' Choice

A Notable Trade Book in the Field of Social Studies

"Best of the Bunch" list, Sydney Taylor Award
Committee/Association of Jewish Libraries

"Perl weaves the history of the Holocaust with a survivor's personal memories of what happened to her family. The writing is direct, devastating, with no rhetoric or exploitation. The truth is in what's said and in what's left out. . . . The personal facts bring it home."

—ALA *Booklist* (starred review)

"This gripping memoir is written in spare, powerful prose that vividly depicts the endless degradation and humiliation suffered by the Holocaust's innocent victims, as well as the unending horror of life in the camps. It's also an ennobling account of the triumph of the human spirit, as seen through a child's eyes."

—*Kirkus Reviews*

"A harrowing and often moving account."

—*School Library Journal*

"Amid a growing number of memoirs about the Holocaust, this book warrants attention both for the uncommon experiences it records and for the fullness of the record."   —*Publishers Weekly*

"Perl collaborates with the three surviving members of the Blumenthal family to tell their moving story. In 1939, four-year-old Marion was interned with her family at the Westerbork camp in Holland; five years later they were imprisoned in the notorious Bergen-Belsen concentration camp. Illustrated with black-and-white photographs, the narrative is interspersed with facts about the rise of Hitler and the progress of the war."   —*The Horn Book*

"Lazan's recollections, along with occasional quotes from her mother, are intertwined with Perl's background narrative to make a smooth factual flow. There's no hint of over-dramatization here; the tone is, if anything, understated, in a story carried by the momentum of history itself. Two inserts of the family and historical photos intensify the poignancy of the account."

—*The Bulletin of the Center for Children's Books*

Marion continues to travel to schools, libraries, churches, and synagogues around the United States, speaking to people of all ages about her Holocaust experiences

INDEX